D0554259

Engel v. Vitale:

PRAYER IN THE SCHOOLS

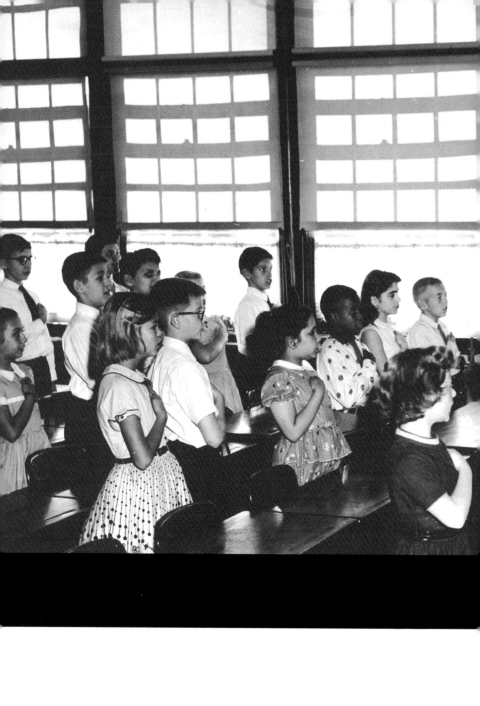

SUPREME COURT MILESTONES

Engel v. Vitale:

Prayer in the Schools

SUSAN DUDLEY GOLD

Marshall Cavendish
Benchmark
New York

To my son, Samuel Bowman Morrison, and my friend, Rosie Wohl, who have always stood firm in defending the First Amendment.

With special thanks to Professor David M. O'Brien of the Woodrow Wilson Department of Politics at the University of Virginia for reviewing the text of this book.

Marshall Cavendish Benchmark · 99 White Plains Road Tarrytown, NY 10591 · www.marshallcavendish.us · Copyright © 2006 by Susan Dudley Gold · All rights reserved. No part of this book may be reproduced or utilized in any form or by any means electronic or mechanical including photocopying, recording, or by any information storage and retrieval system, without permission from the copyright holders.

All Internet sites were available and accurate when sent to press.

Library of Congress Cataloging-in-Publication Data

Gold, Susan Dudley. · Engel v. Vitale : prayer in the schools / by Susan Dudley Gold.— 1st. ed. · p. cm.—(Supreme Court milestones) · Summary: Describes the historical context of the Engel versus Vitale · Supreme Court case, detailing the claims made by both sides as well as the · outcome, and including excerpts from the Supreme Court justices' decisions and relevant sidebars—Provided by publisher. · Includes bibliographical references and index. · ISBN 0-7614-1940-3 · 1. Engel, Steven I.— Trials, litigation, etc.—Juvenile literature. 2. Vitale, William J.—Trials, litigation, etc.— Juvenile literature. 3. Prayer in the public schools—Law and legislation—United States—Juvenile literature. 4. Religion in the public schools—Law and legislation— United States—Juvenile literature. I. Title: Engel versus Vitale. II. Title. III. · Series. · KF228.E54G65 2005 · 344.73'0796—dc22 · 2004025018

Photo Research by Candlepants Incorporated

Cover Photo: Win Mc Namee/Reuters/Corbis

The photographs in this book are used by permission and through the courtesy of: Corbis: Win Mc Namee/Reuters, 1; Bettmann, 20, 28, 33, 41, 74, 102, 105, 107; John Garrett, 109; Gary hershorn/Reuters, 131; Jim Beckel/The Oklahoman, 132; Corbis, 6, 10, 37, 44. *AP/ Wide World Photos*: 2–3, 14, 17, 42, 83, 106. *Law Library Archives, Robert S. Marx Law Library, University of Cincinnati, College of Law*: 85.

Series design by Sonia Chaghatzbanian
Printed in China · 135642

contents

PATRICK HENRY URGED VIRGINIANS TO DECLARE CHRISTIANITY AS THE NATIONAL RELIGION. HIS EFFORTS WERE DEFEATED BY JAMES MADISON AND THOMAS JEFFERSON, AMONG OTHERS.

Foreword

Amendment I, United States Constitution

Congress shall make no law respecting an establishment of religion, or prohibiting the free exercise thereof; or abridging the freedom of speech, or of the press; or the right of the people peaceably to assemble, and to petition the Government for a redress of grievances.

RELIGIOUS FREEDOM is among the most prized of American liberties. The First Amendment guarantees all Americans that freedom. Under the amendment's terms, Congress can neither establish a state-approved religion nor prevent people from practicing their own religion or no religion.

Many of the early European settlers fled from nations with state religions intolerant of other beliefs. They came to America seeking a land where they could observe their faith without interference from the government and state churches. Remembering this history, America's founders resisted pressure to establish a state church in the United States. Patrick Henry, the firebrand patriot from Virginia, led a passionate crusade in the mid–1780s to declare

Christianity as the national religion. But James Madison and Thomas Jefferson—both future presidents—fought off Henry's efforts. Their case for government neutrality served as a basis for the First Amendment.

In opposing Henry's campaign for Christianity, Madison delivered a doctrine that set forth America's commitment to freedom of religion:

> The Religion then of every man must be left to the conviction and conscience of every man; and it is the right of every man to exercise it as these may dictate. This right is in its nature an unalienable right.

For more than two centuries, freedom of religion has remained at the heart of the American way of life. Immigrants from countries all over the world—like the European settlers before them—have come to America's shores to escape from religious persecution and to practice a wide array of religions and ideologies. The "free exercise" section of the First Amendment guarantees the right of these groups to practice their religion as they see fit.

The First Amendment's "establishment clause" bars the government from forming a state church or favoring one church over another. It erects a protective barrier for those with unpopular religious views against pressure from the majority. Despite the founders' commitment to religious neutrality, however, zealots from every corner have sought to win state support for their religious beliefs. Like Patrick Henry, some politicians and their supporters continue to press for a resolution to make the United States a Christian nation. While there are Americans who would overturn the First Amendment's ban on the establishment of a state religion, the majority of citizens reject such a collaboration between government and church.

The real debate is more subtle. It revolves around the question of what is and is not considered "the establishment of religion." Some Americans oppose any connection between the government and religion. They view the First Amendment's freedom of religion guarantee as absolute and believe government has no business promoting or becoming involved with religion in any way. Those holding this view fear that the rights of minorities may be trampled if the government sanctions the religious ceremonies or beliefs practiced by the majority.

Others hold the view that religion has long played a vital role in American life and should be encouraged by the government. These Americans support prayers in school, government subsidies for religious schools, and similar measures. Some of them have attempted to incorporate church icons and rituals—such as the Ten Commandments and the Lord's Prayer—into government-sponsored functions. Court rulings against these efforts, they claim, interfere with their right to exercise their religion freely. They have used this argument to pit the free exercise clause of the First Amendment against the establishment clause.

Another group of Americans oppose government interference or support of religion but believe that long-established religious references have more to do with American tradition and culture than with a particular religion. As such, they contend, these references—such as "In God We Trust" on U.S. coins—are no threat to religious freedom and should remain a part of American heritage.

These conflicting views have resulted in a number of cases that the legal system has addressed. In most cases, the courts have ruled against links between religion and

U.S. COIN DISPLAYING THE NATIONAL MOTTO, "IN GOD WE TRUST."

government as violations of the First Amendment. These cases have sparked a firestorm of protests. The lack of government support for religion, some critics say, has led to moral decay in American society.

The schools became an early battleground over religious freedom. In many areas of the country, public schools were first established by Protestant churches. Students recited prayers and Bible verses as part of the school routine. When local communities assumed responsibility for running the schools, many classrooms continued the religious exercises each morning. In 1958, a school district in Long Island, New York, decided to require students to recite a prayer composed by the State Board of Regents, the body that regulated New York schools. The prayer, which took students about twelve seconds to recite, stirred up strong emotions on both sides of the heated battle over religion and its place in a democracy.

A group of parents who objected to the government-written prayer asked the court to stop the practice. Ultimately, the U.S. Supreme Court would rule on the case, known as *Engel* v. *Vitale*. In its 1962 decision, the Supreme Court ruled that government-sanctioned prayer had no place in public schools. The case became a landmark in the debate over separation of church and state. It marked the first time the Court relied on the establishment clause to bar religious activities at government-sponsored events. Its precepts have been used in cases challenging

religious exercises and ritual in many public settings,
from the Ten Commandments in courthouses to the use of
the phrase "under God" in the Pledge of Allegiance.
Far from "kicking God out of the schools," as
conservatives charged, the decision protected schoolchildren
from government interference with their religion. The
ruling made it clear that children and anyone else can
pray anytime and anywhere. Government, on the other
hand, cannot direct citizens to pray, to read the Bible, or
to perform any other religious activities. The First
Amendment's establishment clause, the Court ruled,
protects all American citizens from such government
intervention in their religious beliefs.

More than a court matter, the debate launched by
Engel has always been a political issue. The decision has
inspired more legislative action than any other U.S.
Supreme Court case. For years members of Congress have
sought to overturn the ruling by passing a constitutional
amendment allowing prayer in public schools. All
attempts have failed so far, but forty-three years after
the Court decided the case, opponents of the *Engel* v.
Vitale decision continue to challenge the ruling. Their
passionate efforts to reinstate prayer in public schools
have made few gains in court but have won support from
conservative politicians.

Equally vehement in their defense of the *Engel*
decision, First Amendment rights groups work as hard to
preserve the separation between church and state. They
believe, as Justice Hugo Black wrote in the *Engel* decision,
that "a union of government and religion tends to destroy
government and to degrade religion."

one
THE REGENTS' PRAYER

MANY U.S. SCHOOLCHILDREN in the 1950s and early 1960s started their mornings by reciting the Pledge of Allegiance and joining together in a short prayer. In public schools in New Hyde Park, New York, teachers led students in a prayer approved by the local school board. New York's State Board of Regents had adopted the prayer—known as the Regents' Prayer—on November 30, 1951, and had recommended that schools in the state use it in their opening rituals each morning. The twenty-two-word prayer read:

> Almighty God, we acknowledge our dependence upon Thee, and we beg Thy blessings upon us, our parents, our teachers and our Country.

After several failed attempts, school board member Mary Harte, who also served as a state regent, won support for her motion that the prayer "be said daily" in the public schools administered by Union Free School District No. 9 (also known as Herricks school system) in New Hyde Park on Long Island. Only board member Philip J. Freed voted against the motion. Following the vote, on July 8, 1958, the board instructed the district principal to have each class recite the prayer after the Pledge of Allegiance every morning.

When school began that fall, teachers taught the new prayer to their students. The teacher, or a student chosen by the teacher, led the class in saying the prayer aloud each day. This daily ritual was followed in all the schools in the district: a senior high school, a junior high school, and five elementary schools, attended by about 5,400 students. Many other schools throughout the state had already included the prayer in their morning ceremonies.

"PUNISHED BY CHRIST"

Lawrence Roth and several other Long Island parents were upset that their children's schools had incorporated a prayer as part of the day's rituals. Roth, who ran a small plastics manufacturing firm, was Jewish, but the family did not practice any religious faith. He did not want his two sons, Joseph, ten, and Daniel, thirteen, to be subjected to a prayer that did not reflect his family's religious views.

"My basic feeling," Roth said later, "was that if the State could tell us what to pray and when to pray and how to pray, there was no stopping."

Roth had encountered other efforts by a teacher at his sons' school to introduce the Christian faith to students. A third-grade teacher kept a statue of Christ in the classroom. "If you were bad," Roth said, "she would say, you would be punished by Christ."

Although teachers did not force anyone to say the Regents' Prayer, students who left the room or did not mouth the words would have been quickly identified as not holding the same beliefs as the majority of the class. Peer pressure convinced students whose families held other religious views to recite the prayer along with everyone else so as not to be labeled different.

Shortly after the prayer had been adopted, Steven

THE CHILDREN AND THEIR PARENTS—WHO SUED TO REMOVE THE REGENTS'
PRAYER FROM NEW YORK SCHOOLS—CELEBRATE THEIR VICTORY AFTER THE
U.S. SUPREME COURT RULED IN THEIR FAVOR IN THE 1962 CASE *ENGEL* V.
VITALE. TOP ROW, FROM LEFT: STUDENTS MICHAEL ENGEL, 11; DAN ROTH, 17;
JUDY LICHTENSTEIN, 19; AND JOE ROTH, 14. SEATED, FROM LEFT: PARENTS
THELMA ENGEL, RUTH LICHTENSTEIN, AND MR. AND MRS. LAWRENCE ROTH.
FRONT, FROM LEFT: CHILDREN JONATHAN ENGEL, 4, AND MADELEINE ENGEL, 7.

Engel, also Jewish, recalled seeing his son "with his hands
clasped and his head bent." He asked the boy what he
was doing. When the child replied that he was saying
his prayers, Engel told him, "That's not the way we say
prayers." Jews, like followers of other religions, have
their own prayers and rituals. Orthodox Jews pray in a
synagogue, and males wear yarmulkes, or head coverings.

When praying, they don't clasp their hands or bow their heads.

Roth believed the Regents' Prayer violated the First Amendment's ban on state-established religion. He contacted the American Civil Liberties Union (ACLU) about the situation. Founded in 1920, the ACLU pledged to defend and preserve the individual rights and liberties of all Americans as guaranteed by the U.S. Constitution. The nonprofit, nonpartisan organization had been a leader in other Bill of Rights struggles.

ALL interested parties

At the urging of the ACLU, Roth set out to find other parents in the district who objected to the prayer. That fall he placed an advertisement in the local paper:

> Notice: To all Herrick's [sic] school district
> taxpayers: A taxpayers suit will soon be
> started to challenge the legality of prayers
> in public schools. Counsel has been appointed.
>
> All interested parties CALL:
> Lawrence Roth
> 555-7652 AFTER 5 P.M. DAILY

Fifty Long Island parents responded to Roth's ad. Like him, they did not think public schools were the place to espouse religious beliefs. Roth and the other parents filed a formal petition asking the school board to discontinue the prayer. When the board members refused, the ACLU agreed to take the parents' concerns to court. The organization's lawyers began preparing a lawsuit challenging the school system's use of the prayer. As the months dragged on, several of the parents withdrew from the campaign because of criticism from friends and clergy. Others were disqualified from a potential lawsuit because their children would have graduated before the courts finally decided the matter. The court considers cases only when a plaintiff is directly affected by a law or action. Once graduated, the children in the case would no longer be exposed to the prayer.

Ultimately, five parents agreed to serve as plaintiffs. A plaintiff is the person or group bringing a complaint before the court. Named as the plaintiffs in the prayer suit were Lawrence Roth, Steven Engel, David Lichtenstein, Monroe Lerner, and Leonore Lyons. Among them, they had ten children who attended the district's schools. Because the plaintiffs were listed alphabetically, Stephen Engel's name appeared first.

The members of the group practiced various faiths: two were Jewish, one was an atheist (a person who denies the existence of God), one attended a Unitarian church, and one belonged to the New York Society for Ethical Culture. The Society for Ethical Culture, founded in 1876, is a religious educational movement that focuses on the worth of each person, with the goal of joining together to create a better world. Followers have no stated belief in God or other religious figures. Although Lawrence Roth was listed in the court papers as an atheist, he described himself later as "a very religious person, but not a churchgoer." Roth said he was born into a Jewish family and had said prayers himself but was "not at all sure" prayers to a higher being accomplished anything. "When affiliation came up," he said of the case, "I explained the way I felt and [our lawyer] said, 'You're the atheist!' Apparently you have to have an atheist in the crowd so we started from there."

On January 22, 1959, the parents' group filed a petition with the New York State Supreme Court asking that the

SIXTH GRADE STUDENTS AT P.S. 116 IN NEW YORK CITY JOIN THEIR TEACHER
IN SALUTING THE FLAG ON OCTOBER 11, 1957.

Regents' Prayer be discontinued. In New York, the supreme
court is the lowest-level court with jurisdiction over such
cases. The petition listed the district school board as
defendants in the case. The name of William J. Vitale Jr.,
as president of the board, headed the list. It was the first
step in a long and involved journey that would eventually
lead to the U.S. Supreme Court and a landmark decision in
the case, which came to be known as *Engel* v. *Vitale.*

TWO
A CONSTITUTION AND A
BILL OF RIGHTS

THE RELIGIONS BROUGHT TO North America by the first European settlers—and the related faiths developed by their descendants—played a central role in American history. The early English colonies were settled by Pilgrims, who had fled from England after breaking with the Church of England, and Puritans, an offshoot of the Church of England with a stricter doctrine. The two groups eventually merged and broke with the Church of England altogether.

There was no separation of church and state. New England Puritan towns looked much like English villages, with a town square and the church in the center. The church was at the center of the settlers' lives as well. New Englanders met with friends and neighbors at the simple white meetinghouse, where both church services and community meetings were held. Church elders held key positions in the community; civic leaders played active roles in the church. The town's selectmen, gathering at the church/meetinghouse, voted on the minister's salary and the upkeep of the building, among other matters. Church officials helped write the town's laws, and judges referred to the Bible as the final authority on legal points.

Just as the church elders in England had been intolerant of the Puritans, the religious leaders in the New England colonies followed a similar course, allowing no dissent from others of different faiths. Only church members could vote in the Massachusetts commonwealth of the 1630s. Laws required everyone to set aside Sunday as a day of rest and religious contemplation. Settlers who failed to follow the tenets of Puritan doctrine were whipped, hanged, or exiled.

religious Dissenters

Despite the harsh treatment meted out to those who did not follow the church's teachings, several of the early settlers objected to Puritan rule. Those who did not agree with Puritan doctrine fled the early colonies and built their own communities. There they practiced their own version of religion. Some allowed other dissenters to share their settlements even if they did not follow the same faith. Roger Williams established a haven for all religions in Rhode Island after Massachusetts Bay Colony leaders ordered the young Welsh preacher to leave in 1635. The document establishing the commonwealth of Rhode Island, issued in 1647, required everyone to obey civil law but decreed that all people "may walk as their consciences persuade them, every one in the name of his God." Puritans referred to Rhode Island as the "sewer of New England" because of its role as a refuge for separatists.

The renowned Quaker William Penn created a haven for followers of his faith and other religions in Pennsylvania, while Lord Baltimore brought his flock of Roman Catholics to Maryland. Swedish and Dutch settlers in New York and nearby areas established their own churches in that region.

Each ethnic group brought its own language and culture to the New World settlements, and each followed its own faith. By the mid–1600s, more than twenty languages were spoken in New York alone. Eventually, there were so many different religions that no one sect could claim control.

At the end of the French and Indian Wars in 1763, Britain gained control of Canada and of all North American lands east of the Mississippi River except Florida and New Orleans. The Protestant British soon decreed that the Church of England would be the official church in the new territory and began setting up schools to teach children the doctrines of the faith.

ROGER WILLIAMS WAS BANISHED FROM THE MASSACHUSETTS BAY COLONY IN 1635 BECAUSE OF RELIGIOUS DIFFERENCES. HE ESTABLISHED THE COMMONWEALTH OF RHODE ISLAND, WHERE PEOPLE OF MANY FAITHS FOUND REFUGE.

GOVERNMENT BY THE PEOPLE

The colonists in the territory that would soon become the United States of America had no intention of allowing the British to dictate their religion, or anything else. Within twelve years, they revolted against British rule and formed a new nation. A remarkable Constitution established a unique government controlled by the people.

During the American Revolution, leaders of the rebellion drew up the Articles of Confederation to unite their followers. The document formed a loose union of thirteen states and gave the federal government the power to wage the war. Each state retained "sovereignty, freedom, and independence, and every power, jurisdiction, and right" not specifically delegated to the federal government.

Following the American Revolution, the new nation continued to operate as a confederation of strong, independent states. Without a war to unify them, however, the states pulled in many different directions. Under the Articles of Confederation, the federal government had no power to enforce laws, levy taxes, or perform other duties unless all the states agreed.

It became apparent, at least to many leaders, that to survive the nation would have to establish a strong federal government. With the fight for independence still fresh in their minds, these men wanted assurances that those in more powerful states would not restrict the freedoms of other Americans. To guarantee freedom for all, delegates from the thirteen former colonies met to draw up a written constitution, listing the rights and responsibilities of every citizen. The novel document these founders produced became the U.S. Constitution, today the world's oldest written constitution.

Religious freedom was among the most pressing concerns of these leaders. They wanted to ensure that the religious rights of their constituents would not be trampled. The fifty-five delegates who met at the Constitutional Convention in Philadelphia in May 1787 were of many faiths. They represented a population of four million, consisting of followers of dozens of Protestant sects, approximately 25,000 Catholics, and 10,000 Jews, as well as a majority of citizens who professed no religious affiliation.

It was no surprise that most of the delegates to the convention opposed the establishment of a national church. Even leaders who might have favored such a church opposed the measure because they feared delegates might select a religion other than their own. Quakers, Mennonites, Amish, and other groups opposed to the use of force took a strong stand to separate church from state. This was a revolutionary idea; all the European nations had state churches.

NO POSITION ON RELIGION

To win broad support from delegates to the Constitutional Convention, the authors of the Constitution avoided almost all religious references. As a result, the U.S. Constitution makes no mention of God or of the relationship between church and state. Under the Constitution, the incoming president can either swear or affirm the oath of office. The founders provided this choice for those who, like Roger Williams, refused to swear a religious oath for a civil duty. Furthermore, Article VI of the Constitution states that "no religious Test shall ever be required as a Qualification to any Office or public Trust under the United States." Charles Pinckney, a South Carolina delegate, proposed that wording to prevent future discrimination against people who did not hold the religious beliefs of those in power. At the time, several states required office holders to be of a certain religion.

Pinckney also suggested adding a clause that would ban Congress from interfering in religious disputes. The delegates gave little support to the measure, and it failed. Some delegates, most notably James Madison, the main author of the Constitution, argued that such a clause was unnecessary because such activity was so obviously not allowed in a democracy. Other delegates believed that if the Constitution banned one action regarding religion, Congress might try to take other actions not specifically mentioned in the document. It was better, they argued, to leave all mention of religion out of the Constitution.

The Constitutional Convention eventually approved the Constitution without any reference to a particular religion. It became effective on March 4, 1789, after nine states ratified the document. Before agreeing to ratify the Constitution, delegates in New York and Virginia pressed for a separate Bill of Rights that guaranteed individual liberties. To win support for the Constitution, the national delegates accepted a compromise that would add a bill of rights to the original document. Religious freedom was first on the list of liberties to be included.

LIKE THE SPANISH INQUISITION

Many Americans felt uneasy about leaving the relationship between religion and government open to interpretation. The behavior of religious activists like Patrick Henry reinforced their belief that a written document guaranteeing religious liberty was needed. Henry had become known as the orator of the Revolution after he forcefully urged his fellow Virginians to arm themselves against the British in 1775. His plea ended with the immortal words, "I know not what course others may take; but as for me, give me liberty or give me death."

Henry proposed a general assessment bill in the Virginia legislature in 1784 that would have taxed the state's citizens to pay for "the support of Christian teachers" and various Christian churches. The legislation, titled "A Bill Establishing a Provision for Teachers of the Christian Religion," would not have provided funds for Jews and others of non-Christian faiths. Supporters of the bill, mostly of the Anglican faith, argued that Christianity provided the "best means of promoting Virtue, Peace, and Prosperity." Baptists and some Presbyterians opposed the bill because they believed that government support threatened to corrupt religion. They favored a strict separation between civic matters and religious practices.

Madison, a firm believer in the separation of church and state, compared the bill to the Spanish Inquisition, during which those who were not true to the Roman Catholic faith were tortured by the Spanish authorities. "It differs from it [the Inquisition] only in degree," Madison wrote. "The one is the first step, the other the last in the career of intolerance."

He and Thomas Jefferson, author of the Declaration of Independence, led opposition to the bill. Madison outlined his position in his "Memorial and Remonstrance Against Religious Assessments":

> The religion then of every man must be left to the conviction and conscience of every man; and it is the right of every man to exercise it as these may dictate. This right is in its nature an unalienable right.

> It is unalienable, because the opinions of men, depending only on the evidence contemplated by their own minds, cannot follow the dictates of other men: It is unalienable also, because what is here a right towards men, is a duty towards the Creator. It is the duty of every man to render to the Creator such homage, and such only, as he believes to be acceptable to him.

"Who does not see," Madison asked those considering Henry's bill, "that the same authority which can establish Christianity, in exclusion of all other Religions, may establish with the same ease any particular sect of Christianity, in exclusion of all other Sects?"

Swayed by such powerful arguments, the Virginia legislature defeated the bill and, in 1786, adopted instead Jefferson's Bill for Establishing Religious Freedom. It read in part:

No man shall be compelled to frequent or support any religious worship, place, or ministry whatsoever, nor shall be enforced, restrained, molested, or burthened in his body or goods, nor shall otherwise suffer, on account of his religious opinions or belief; but that all men shall be free to profess, and by argument to maintain, their opinions in matters of religion.

First Amendment

Madison drew upon Jefferson's bill and his own arguments when he wrote the First Amendment. The first draft read, "The civil rights of none shall be abridged on account of religious belief, nor shall any national religion be established, nor shall the full and equal rights of conscience in any manner or on any pretext be infringed." Alexander Hamilton, among others, criticized Madison's effort as being too specific. Hamilton used the same arguments posed against Pinckney's proposal: Any restriction not specified might be employed later to deprive people of their religious liberty.

The final form of the First Amendment contained more general language: "Congress shall make no law respecting an establishment of religion, or prohibiting the free exercise thereof." The first part of the amendment banned the federal government from establishing a national church or officially favoring one religion or church over another. This became known as the "establishment clause." The second part of the amendment, known as the "free exercise clause," barred federal authorities from interfering in people's religious practices. This was followed by guarantees of the freedom of speech and the press and the right to assemble peaceably and to petition the government.

The full paragraph, along with nine other amendments to the Constitution, became the Bill of Rights. Passed by Congress on September 25, 1789, and ratified by the states in less than three months, these ten amendments serve as the centerpiece of individual American liberties. The fact that the Bill of Rights begins with a guarantee of religious freedom demonstrates how strongly the founders valued that particular liberty.

Haven of Religious Freedom

When George Washington took office as the nation's first president in 1789, Moses Seixas, the warden of Newport, Rhode Island's Jewish congregation, wrote to congratulate the new leader and to extol the new nation as one that would ensure the congregation's "invaluable rights as free citizens." This new U.S. government of the people, he said, was an institution "which to bigotry gives no sanction, to persecution no assistance."

Washington borrowed Seixas's words to assure Baptists, Jews, Roman Catholics, Quakers, and others who did not practice the mainstream religions of the time that the United States would be a haven of religious freedom and not just tolerance:

> All possess alike liberty of conscience and immunities of citizenship. It is now no more that

toleration is spoken of, as if it was by the indulgence of one class of people that another enjoyed the exercise of their inherent natural rights. For happily the Government of the United States, which gives to bigotry no sanction, to persecution no assistance, requires only that they who live under its protection should demean themselves as good citizens, in giving it on all occasions their effectual support.

Washington was a member of Christ Church in Alexandria, Virginia, although he rarely attended services. Like many of America's founders, including Jefferson and Madison, he held deist views. That means that though Washington believed in God, he did not follow the teachings of any established church.

Washington, however, was not a purist when it came to separation of church and state. His actions illustrated the complexity of the religious question and the entwinement of religion and politics. Despite his deist views and his belief in religious liberty, the first president frequently mingled religious activities and official acts of state. Responding to a request from Congress, Washington proclaimed as one of his first acts of office a day of national thanksgiving and prayer. The National Thanksgiving Proclamation noted that "it is the duty of all nations to acknowledge the providence of Almighty God, to obey His will, to be grateful for His benefits, and humbly to implore His protection and favor."

Washington approved public funds to pay religious leaders to lead Congress in prayer at the beginning of each session. He also consented to put armed services chaplains on the public payroll.

John Adams, the nation's second president, followed a similar course. In his inaugural speech in 1797,

PENNSYLVANIA: A PRIMER.   75

The FRAME of the
GOVERNMENT
OF THE
Province of **Pennsilvania**
IN
A M E R I C A :
Together with certain
L A W S
Agreed upon in England
BY THE
GOVERNOUR
AND
Divers F.R.E E- M E N of the aforesaid
PROVINCE.

To be further Explained and Confirmed there by the firſt
Provincial Council and *General Aſſembly* that ſhall
be held, if they ſee meet.

Printed in the Year MDCLXXXII.
FAC-SIMILE OF TITLE PAGE OF PENN'S "FRAME OF GOVERNMENT, 1682."

THE COLONIAL CONSTITUTION OF PENNSYLVANIA,
1682. WILLIAM PENN OPENED PENNSYLVANIA TO
QUAKERS AND MEMBERS OF OTHER RELIGIONS.

the second president noted his "veneration" for Christianity and said "a decent respect" for that religion was "among the best recommendations for the public service." Nevertheless, Adams expressed deist views and supported the separation of church and state. In one of the early acts of his presidency, Adams presented a treaty with Tripoli to the U.S. Senate for ratification. Pledging peace and friendship with the Muslim African nation, the treaty was negotiated to reduce pirates' attacks on U.S. sailors. It began, "As the government of the United States . . . is not in any sense founded on the Christian religion. . . ." The Senate unanimously approved the treaty in 1797. Its publication on the front pages of the newspapers of the time did not appear to trigger any controversy.

Adams later blamed his defeat at the polls on his push for a national fast. In March 1799 he had asked Congress to declare April 25 as "a day of solemn humiliation, fasting, and prayer." He recognized, too late, that the voters opposed such governmental interference in religion: "Nothing is more dreaded than the national government meddling with religion," he wrote in an 1812 letter to Benjamin Rush.

A NATURAL RIGHT

Thomas Paine, whose writings in a pamphlet called *Common Sense* helped ignite the American Revolution, was a severe critic of organized religion. He wrote in his book *Age of Reason* of the "wonderful structure of the universe" and based his faith on the miracle of creation. Like many others of different faiths, Paine touted his religious belief (deism) as "the only true religion." Nevertheless, he just as firmly believed in religious freedom. Religion, he noted in his "Rights of Man," is one of the "natural rights" a person is born with.

Thomas Jefferson and Benjamin Franklin, who also held deist views, argued that establishment of a state church would threaten the nation's newly won independence. Jefferson in particular resisted handing over power to religious leaders, whom he believed used their position to abuse power. "In every country and in every age, the priest has been hostile to liberty," he wrote in a letter to Horatio Spafford in 1814. "He is always in alliance with the despot, abetting his abuses in return for protection to his own."

Unlike Washington and Adams, Jefferson adamantly refused to issue any religious proclamations during his term in office. "I know it will give great offense to the clergy," he said of his decision, "but the advocate of religious freedom is to expect neither peace nor forgiveness from them." During his two runs for the presidency, the opposing political party, the Federalists, tried to paint Jefferson as an atheist because of his views on the separation of church and state. The opposition claimed that made him unfit to serve as president.

Jefferson used his reply to a letter from the Connecticut Baptists Association of Danbury as a vehicle to fight the charges of his political enemy. Connecticut law at the time required citizens of that state to pay the salaries of ministers of the Congregational and Presbyterian churches, the denominations with the most followers. According to the law, those of other faiths could avoid paying the tax if they produced a letter from their own church stating that they paid an equal sum toward the minister's upkeep. As followers of a minority religion, the Baptists objected to this practice and asked for religious liberty:

> Our Sentiments are uniformly on the side of Religious Liberty—That religion is at all times and places a matter between God and Individuals— That no man ought to suffer in Name, person or effects on account of his religious Opinions—That the legitimate Power of Civil Government extends no further than to punish the man who works ill to his neighbor . . .
>
> What religious privileges we enjoy (as a minor part of the State) we enjoy as favor granted, and not as inalienable rights: And these favors we receive at the expense of such degrading acknowledgements, as are inconsistent with the rights of freemen.

In his reply to the letter, Jefferson—like Washington— reassured the Baptists of his support for religious freedom. He reiterated the strong prohibitions against such activities contained in the First Amendment's religion clauses. These two clauses, Jefferson wrote, built "a wall of separation between Church & State." This phrase, used in more than one Supreme Court ruling on religion, became the watchword of guardians of religious liberty.

Religious Persecution

Even with as powerful an advocate as Jefferson, religious freedom remained limited for those not practicing mainstream Protestantism. States claimed the right to determine their own policies when it came to religion. Official state churches, supported by taxpayers, continued to operate in Massachusetts, Connecticut, New Hampshire, and Maryland. Until 1833, Massachusetts taxpayers paid the salaries of instructors hired to teach the Protestant religion. Connecticut tax dollars supported the Congregational church until 1868.

Money wasn't the only issue. States discriminated against—and in some cases persecuted—those who were not mainstream Protestants. Only Protestants had the full rights of citizens in New Jersey until the law changed in 1844. New Hampshire did not allow Jews or Catholics to vote until 1851. Another twenty-five years passed before members of those faiths could hold public office in the state. Jews and Unitarians did not have full civil rights in Maryland until 1876.

In the 1830s and 1840s, the Mormons, members of the Church of Jesus Christ of Latter-Day Saints, trekked from New York to Ohio to Missouri to escape violent opposition to their faith. Their religion permitted Mormon men to marry more than one wife, a practice known as polygamy.

That belief clashed with the views of the majority of Americans. No state would accept them. Missouri officials threatened to wipe out the sect. In Illinois, an outraged mob dragged Mormon founder Joseph Smith from jail and murdered him. On October 8, 1845, Mormon leader Brigham Young led his flock of sixteen thousand on a two-year journey across the wilderness to Utah, then owned by Mexico. The sect settled there in the Great Salt Lake Basin.

Although Jews first came to North America in 1654, they remained a tiny minority until a large group migrated from Germany in the early 1800s and thousands more fled to the United States in the decades following the Civil War. The potato famine in Ireland in the 1840s and new farming techniques that displaced thousands of Eastern European peasants in mid-century brought tens of thousands of Roman Catholics to America. Between 1847 and 1874, nine thousand Chinese laborers came to the United States to work on the Transcontinental Railroad.

These new immigrants began to change the religious makeup of the United States. Those who feared losing power to Catholics and other religious groups tried to shut the doors to newcomers. An anti-Catholic group, the American Protective Association (a precursor of the Ku Klux Klan), declared that followers of "any ecclesiastical power not created and controlled by American citizens"— the Catholic pope, for example—should not be allowed to become U.S. citizens.

Beginning in the 1830s, Nativists—those who wanted to close America to all those born in any other country— churned out letters, books, and articles denouncing foreigners. Samuel F. B. Morse, inventor of the telegraph and a leading Nativist, urged Congress to halt immigration altogether and described Catholicism as "hostile in its very nature to republican liberty."

These views stirred up hatred against immigrants, which erupted into violence in some areas. In 1844, rioters led by Nativists ravaged Philadelphia streets, burning two Catholic churches and destroying homes in Irish Catholic neighborhoods. The mob killed more than twenty people. Such incidents, however, did little to curb the growing immigrant population and the increasing numbers of non-Protestants arriving in America. For example, in 1840 about 45 percent of the population in Cincinnati, Ohio, was foreign born. Many of the newcomers were German Jews and Catholics. Nationally, by 1850, Roman Catholicism claimed more members than any other faith in America.

Mobs attacked Irish Catholics during riots in New York on July 12, 1871. Religious differences between Protestants and Catholics led to violence in many cities during the mid–1800s.

"DON'T BELIEVE IN THAT"

An 1871 dispute in a public school at Hunters Point in Long Island, New York, illustrates the clash between Catholics and Protestants in the nineteenth century. At the time, the bylaws of the New York Department of Education required the state's public schools to include Bible readings and religious songs in their opening exercises. Both were based on Protestant teachings.

When a Catholic school trustee objected to this practice, the school board voted to suspend the reading for one month. At the end of that time, the board voted to have school officials read either the Ten Commandments or the Lord's Prayer to their students.

Again the trustee, Joseph Frisel, objected and urged the board to eliminate all religious exercises at the school.

When the principal began reading the Lord's Prayer (the Protestant version) the following week, a Catholic student stood up and shouted, "Don't believe in that." She was suspended, but the next day she repeated her protest. Three young men who tried to prevent the principal from ejecting her were arrested and taken to the local jail.

According to an article about the incident in *The New York Times*, the principal "was hooted at in the streets, and on several occasions was pelted with stones." Catholic students continued their protest at the school. After thirty-two students shouted, "Don't believe in that," during the principal's recitation of the Lord's Prayer, school officials suspended them. Later, police confronted angry parents who came to the school to get their children reinstated.

The New York Times account of the episode blamed the local priest for the disturbance. "Throughout the entire day a battle raged between parents determined to carry out the instructions of their violent priest," the obviously

34

ised report read. The reporter went on to accuse th[e] [pr]iest of "preaching destruction to the Bible."

Although conceding that "logically and legally there [was] [so]mething to say from their side of the matter," th[e] [re]porter further chastised the Catholic protestors. "It do[es] [seem] incredible in the nineteenth century," he wrot[e,] [t]hat the Catholics cannot try this question calmly an[d] [dis]passionately in the courts of law."

OUR EDUCATORS.

THE READING OF THE BIBLE IN THE SCHOOLS.

AMERICAN SCHOOL COMMISSIONER. "But, my good Sir, we have always read the Bible in our American Schools ever since the first settlement of the country."

IRISH SCHOOL COMMISSIONER. "Worse luck, thin; ye'll rade it no more! Father O'Flaherty says it interfares wid our holy religion, an' by the Vargin it won't and it shan't be read!"

POLITICAL CARTOON OF THE 1800S CRITICIZING CATHOLIC OBJECTIONS [TO] [TH]E READING OF THE PROTESTANT BIBLE IN THE SCHOOLS. THE CATHOLI[C]

A FAITH OF THEIR OWN

These new Americans did not want their children to be indoctrinated in a faith not their own. Like the early settlers before them, they wanted to be able to follow their own religious tenets. In 1843, Jewish parents complained about lessons from the New Testament of the Bible that were being taught in the public schools in New York City. The school board supported the teachings as a way to "inculcate general principles of Christianity." Rabbi Isaac Mayer Wise, a Jewish leader in Cincinnati, commented on Protestant ministers' insistence that schools in that city continue Bible readings. "It is a shame," he wrote, "that those reverend gentlemen cannot attend to their own business, to teach religion to their flock, and want the teachers of the public school to assist them, to do the business for which they are paid."

Catholics also objected to Bible readings in the public schools. Members of that faith used the Douay-Rheims Bible, not the King James version favored by Protestants and from which the readings were derived. Their objections were met with ridicule and violence. The Philadelphia riots, in fact, erupted as a result of the demands by Catholic parents that the schools stop reading the Protestant Bible to their children.

FOURTEENTH AMENDMENT

Early court battles supported states' rights to determine religious issues. An 1845 ruling by the U.S. Supreme Court, in *Permoli* v. *Municipality No. 1 of City of New Orleans*, clearly gave states the power to regulate religion. According to the decision, written by Justice John Catron,

the Bill of Rights barred only the *federal* government
from interfering with religion. "The Constitution makes
no provision for protecting the citizens of the respective
states in their religious liberties," the opinion read; "this
is left to the state constitutions and laws."

That changed with the passage of the Fourteenth
Amendment. The Amendment, passed by Congress in
1866 and ratified by the states in 1868, placed limits
on the states. Section 1 of the amendment spelled out
three restrictions:

- The states could not deny citizens the privileges
  guaranteed them in the Constitution.
- The states could not take away life, liberty, or
  property without "due process"; that is, a state
  had to follow certain procedures before it could
  put a citizen to death, interfere with his or her
  liberty, or take away his or her property. This is
  known as the "due process clause."
- The states had to treat people equally.

In arguing for passage of the Fourteenth Amendment,
Senator Jacob Howard of Michigan said its purpose
was to protect citizens' rights against states' power.
"The great object of the first section of this amendment
is, therefore, to restrain the power of the states and
compel them at all times to respect these fundamental
rights."

Although states continued to claim exemption from
the Bill of Rights, the courts in a growing number
of cases ruled against them, based on the Fourteenth
Amendment.

THree
FIRST AMENDMENT ON TRIAL

For more than two Hundred years, the First Amendment has been the protector of American freedoms. The first sixteen words of the amendment guarantee religious liberty. These two clauses preserve Americans' religious rights in two ways: the right to "free exercise" of their own religion and the right to be free from state-imposed religion (the "establishment" clause). Court cases involving religious freedom focus on one or both of these rights.

BeLiefs and practices: THe free Exercise clause

The right to exercise religion freely lies at the core of what it means to be an American. Whether this phrase covers religious practices as well as beliefs has been the subject of much debate. Courts have ruled one way on the issue, only to reverse judgment in later cases.

In an 1878 case, *Reynolds* v. *United States*, the Supreme Court ruled that the free exercise clause applied only to religious beliefs and did not extend to religious practices. The case involved the Mormon practice of polygamy, having more than one spouse at a time. In upholding the federal law banning polygamy, the Court ruled that while laws "cannot interfere with mere religious belief and opinions, they may with practices."

Two years later, in the 1890 case *Davis* v. *Beason*, the Court further narrowed its definition of religious liberty. The ruling unanimously upheld the conviction of an Idaho man, Samuel D. Davis, for falsely taking an oath that he was not a Mormon in order to vote. Idaho denied the vote to anyone who advocated or practiced polygamy or belonged to an organization that did. Davis himself neither promoted not practiced polygamy. Nevertheless, the Court denied his appeal on the grounds that *religion* refers only to "one's views of his relations to his Creator, and to the obligations they impose." Religious practices, on the other hand, must not threaten "the peace and safety of the state," according to the Court. "However free the exercise of religion may be," the decision read, "it must be subordinate to the criminal laws of the country, passed with reference to actions regarded by general consent as properly the subjects of punitive legislation."

"The Greater Good"

The Court reiterated the opinion that the state's "peace and safety" outweighed religious beliefs in a 1940s case, *Minersville School District* v. *Gobitis*. Officials at the Minersville Public School System in the hills of east-central Pennsylvania expelled William and Lillian Gobitas in 1935. The children had refused to participate in the daily school exercise of reciting the Pledge of Allegiance and saluting the American flag. Their parents said such a requirement violated their beliefs as Jehovah's Witnesses.

Jehovah's Witnesses believe that the Lord's instructions in the Bible forbid them from saluting a flag—a graven image in their view. Ten-year-old William described his belief in a letter to school authorities:

Dear Sirs, I do not salute the flag because
I have promised to do the will of God.

That means that I must not worship anything
out of harmony with God's law. In the twentieth
chapter of Exodus it is stated, "Thou shalt not
make unto thee any graven image, nor bow down
to them nor serve them. . . ." I do not salute the
flag [not] because I do not love my country,
but [because] I love my country and I love God
more and I must obey His commandments.
—Your pupil, Billy Gobitas

(Gobitas is the correct spelling of the name.
Unfortunately, it was spelled Gobitis in the initial legal
documents. The misspelling remained in the Supreme
Court case title and most subsequent sources.)

Olin R. Moyle, the Witnesses' attorney, argued the
Gobitas case before Judge Albert Maris of the U.S. District
Court for the Eastern District of Pennsylvania. Moyle
claimed the Minersville School Board had no right to force
the children to violate their religious beliefs since the flag
salute "does not and cannot affect the public interest or
safety of others."

Judge Maris ruled in favor of the Gobitas children. On
June 18, 1938, he ordered the school district to re-enroll
the children and not to require them to salute the flag.

The school board appealed to the Court of Appeals for
the Third Circuit. The three-judge panel ruled for the
Gobitases. In the opinion, the panel noted that Adolf
Hitler, then in power in Germany, persecuted Jehovah's
Witnesses and confiscated their property and literature.
The judges cited the history of religious persecution in the
founding of the colonies and in Pennsylvania in particular.
The opinion concluded by quoting George Washington:
"I assure you very explicitly, that in my opinion the
conscientious scruples of all men should be treated with
great delicacy and tenderness."

WALTER GOBITAS, CENTER, AND HIS TWO CHILDREN, WILLIAM AND LILLIAN, LEAVE THE U.S. DISTRICT COURT IN PHILADELPHIA AFTER THE STUDENTS TESTIFIED THAT SALUTING THE FLAG VIOLATED THEIR RELIGIOUS BELIEFS AS JEHOVAH'S WITNESSES.

Not willing to give up, the school board took the case to the U.S. Supreme Court. In an eight to one decision, the Court ruled against the Gobitases. Justice Felix Frankfurter, writing for the majority, emphasized the need to bow to the greater good in promoting national unity over religious freedom. The law requiring children to recite the pledge was an important way to unite the country, which in turn was "the basis of national security," Frankfurter said. Religious beliefs did not excuse citizens from obeying the law, he added. Such necessary "adjustment" to comply with government regulations had not violated religious freedom, the justice concluded.

Frankfurter was held in such high esteem by the other justices that all but one voted with him on the case, even though several would later express regret at their position. Justices Hugo Black, William O. Douglas, Owen J. Roberts, Stanley Reed, and Frank Murphy would vote to overturn the decision just three years later.

Patriotism was much on the minds of the nation's leaders in 1940. Many people considered the disruptive labor movement in the United States to be influenced by Communists backed by the Soviet Union. The growing threat of Hitler's Germany also encouraged nationalistic sentiments. Many people viewed a refusal to salute the flag as a threat to national security.

U.S. SUPREME COURT JUSTICE FELIX FRANKFURTER HOLDS A LAW BOOK IN HIS OFFICE IN WASHINGTON, D.C., ON NOV. 14, 1957. FRANKFURTER SUFFERED A STROKE AFTER THE ORAL ARGUMENTS IN *ENGEL* WERE HEARD, AND DID NOT VOTE ON THE CASE.

Justice Harlan F. Stone, the lone dissenter in *Gobitis*, argued that the Minersville law suppressed freedom of speech and freedom of religion, a violation of both the First and the Fourteenth amendments. Not only that, but the state "seeks to coerce these children to express a sentiment which . . . violates their deepest religious convictions." Stone said that, historically, governments that suppressed individual liberties usually justified their actions by claiming to support the public good. Most of these attempts, he noted, were directed "at politically helpless minorities"—like the Jehovah's Witnesses.

The Constitution guarantees "freedom of the human mind and spirit," Stone asserted, and this must be preserved at all costs:

> The very essence of the liberty which they [the Constitution's provisions] guarantee is the freedom of the individual from compulsion as to what he shall think and what he shall say, at least where the compulsion is to bear false witness to his religion. If these guarantees are to have any meaning they must, I think . . . withhold from the state any authority to compel belief or the expression of it where that expression violates religious convictions, whatever may be the legislative view of the desirability of such compulsion.

Stone questioned how forcing children to say what they didn't believe could promote national unity. Allowing a law that required such actions, the justice continued, amounted to "the surrender of the constitutional protection of the liberty of small minorities to the popular will." It was precisely the

ADOLF HITLER ORDERED A BOYCOTT OF JEWISH MERCHANTS BEGINNING APRIL 1, 1933, AS PART OF THE NAZI PARTY'S DEADLY CAMPAIGN AGAINST JEWS. THE PLACARD ON A JEWISH STORE IN BERLIN READS: "GERMANS, DEFEND YOURSELVES, DO NOT BUY FROM JEWS."

role of the courts, he said, to prevent mob rule from trampling the rights of powerless minorities.

The *Gobitis* decision unleashed a series of violent attacks against Jehovah's Witnesses. Mobs shot at Witnesses, beat them, and tarred and feathered them. Their cars, homes, and meeting halls were burned. Enemies spread rumors that the Witnesses were spies trying to sabotage America. Schools across the country expelled the Witnesses' children for not saluting the flag.

However, newspaper editorials expressed outrage over the Supreme Court decision, and a number of political leaders criticized the ruling. As stories of the Witnesses' persecution spread, the nation's courts, if not its people, began to view the sect's claims more sympathetically. Usually, lower courts are guided by Supreme Court opinions. This time, however, court after court ignored the *Gobitis* ruling and directed that Witnesses' children be allowed to attend school unmolested without saluting the flag.

In 1943, in the case of *West Virginia State Board of Education* v. *Barnette*, the U.S. Supreme Court overturned the *Gobitis* decision. Now, with Stone as chief justice, the Court voted six to three in favor of the Witnesses. Like the Gobitas children, Marie Barnette had been expelled from school for not saluting the flag. The Court announced its decision on Flag Day, June 14, 1943. Frankfurter led the dissent, again noting that such issues should be decided by the states, not the courts.

In his opinion for the majority, Justice Robert H. Jackson reiterated the views in Justice Stone's dissent. Such actions by the state, he wrote, violated the Constitution:

> If there is any fixed star in our constitutional
> constellation, it is that no official, high or petty,

can prescribe what shall be orthodox in politics, nationalism, religion, or other matters of opinion or force citizens to confess by word or act of faith therein. . . . We think the action of the local authorities in compelling the flag salute and pledge transcends constitutional limitations on their power and invades the sphere of intellect and spirit which it is the purpose of the First Amendment to our Constitution to reserve from all official control.

There was no repeat of the violent attacks against the Witnesses after the *Barnette* decision was read. The horrors revealed in Nazi Germany served as a caution against the excesses of national unity and religious bigotry. People began to see the difference between forced salutes and concentration camps as only one of degree.

The *Barnette* decision has remained the primary bulwark against restrictions on the free exercise of religion in the United States.

STATES' INTERESTS V. INDIVIDUAL RIGHTS

Another important Supreme Court case helped clarify the conflict between states' interests and individual rights. In some instances, the states' interests—for example in educating children—can be so important that they can override an individual's rights. But that happens only if the state can prove there is no other way to accomplish its goals.

The case of *Wisconsin* v. *Yoder* began with Jonas Yoder, a traditional Amish farmer in Wisconsin. The Amish, a religious community in existence for more than three hundred years, believe in keeping to themselves and shunning modern conveniences, such as cars, telephones, and computers. Their way of life is similar to that of nineteenth century farming communities.

Yoder protested a Wisconsin state law requiring children to attend school until the age of sixteen. Like other Amish parents, he allowed his children to go to public school only through eighth grade. Older Amish children stay at home and learn basic farming skills such as carpentry, tanning, and weaving.

Wisconsin authorities fined Yoder and other Amish parents who did not send their older children to school. The Amish believed this was a restriction of their religious freedom. Not only did it interfere with their way of life, they said, but it risked their children's heavenly salvation by teaching them sinful ways of the modern world. Yoder and two other Amish families took the matter to court.

When *Wisconsin* v. *Yoder* reached the Supreme Court in 1972, the Amish pleaded to be allowed to practice their religion and preserve their way of life. They contended that the state, by fining them, had violated their First Amendment rights to express their religion freely.

The Court found that the Amish parents' way of life was firmly connected to their deeply held religious beliefs. The First and Fourteenth amendments protected their right to express those beliefs. In addition, the Court agreed that the Amish did a good job of preparing their children for life in their community. Therefore, the Court concluded, the state's interest in requiring one or two more years of formal education was not compelling enough to override Yoder's religious freedom.

In the majority opinion, Chief Justice Warren Burger wrote that only when a state's interests were "of the highest order" and could not be "otherwise served" would that state be permitted to restrict religious liberties. The Amish situation did not fit into this category, but human sacrifice, for example, would not be allowed, even if it were part of a church's sacraments.

ESTABLISHMENT CLAUSE: SEPARATION OF CHURCH AND STATE

The *Barnette* and *Yoder* cases helped establish the boundaries of free exercise of religion. Several other Court decisions have dealt with the First Amendment's ban on government's establishment of religion. Controversy over the ban, however, continues unabated. What some view as a violation of their First Amendment rights, others consider a part of their heritage. Court rulings on the conflict have been mixed. This reflects the deep divide between those who view some religious observances as long-entrenched customs that should be preserved and those who believe such activities represent an "establishment of religion" by the government.

The establishment clause lay at the heart of a case involving Bible reading in the public schools of Cincinnati. In 1869, nearly twelve thousand Cincinnati students attended private Catholic schools. In an effort to strengthen the public school system, local officials tried to convince those students to attend the city's schools. As part of a compromise with Catholics, who objected to the King James version of the Bible, the Cincinnati school board proposed a ban on Bible readings and religious teachings in the public schools. Under the agreement, the city would take over some Catholic school buildings, and Catholic students would transfer to public schools. The proposal outraged pro-Bible forces. They saw it as "a devilish Catholic plot to remove the Bible from the public schools, leaving the students of these godless institutions devoid of moral direction and religious instruction."

The Catholic bishop eventually withdrew his support for the plan, but the board continued discussion of the Bible ban. At a mass rally, Rufus King, a former school board president and one of the lawyers who would later argue the case in court, told an enraged crowd that having no public schools would be far better than running "the 'godless' institutions which they would thus become." The newspapers quickly dubbed the conflict "the Bible Wars."

Despite fierce opposition, the school board voted 22 to 15 to pass the ban. The next day a court halted the ban temporarily at the request of Bible supporters. The case, *Minor* v. *Board of Education of Cincinnati*, eventually reached the Ohio Supreme Court. It became an early landmark case in the battle over religion in the public schools.

J. P. Stallo, who represented the school board in the battle, argued that Jews and others of non-Christian faiths had been unjustly tarred as "atheists and infidels" by the pro-Bible supporters. "If they have equal civil rights with the orthodox Christians, the Bible must of necessity be excluded from the State schools, and sent to the Christian houses, Sunday schools, and churches. There are no civil rights exclusive to Christian believers, nor any rights, including the right of conscience, that they legally can be denied."

Stallo issued the assurance that removing the Bible from the classroom would not result in the end of the world or produce an epidemic of immorality. The churches, he noted, would still provide religious training, and people could freely read the Bible.

The court agreed, issuing a unanimous ruling in 1873 to reinstate the Bible ban. The ruling did not ban Bible reading elsewhere, but it gave local school boards the power to decide the issue. It also rejected the premise that Christianity was the religion of the United States and firmly supported the separation of church and state:

> [Christianity's] laws are divine, and not human. Its essential interests lie beyond the reach and range of human governments. United with government, religion never rises above the merest superstition; united with religion, government never rises above the merest despotism; and all history shows us that the more widely and completely they are separated, the better it is for both.

In the decision, the court reinforced the opinion of the lower court judge, Alphonso Taft, who noted that the Constitution did not permit schools run and paid for by the government to promote "Protestant worship." For the first time the court ruled that Bible reading and the claim that America was a Christian nation conflicted with the First Amendment's insistence that government not favor any particular religion.

The Illinois Supreme Court addressed the same issue in a 1910 case, *Ring* v. *Board of Education*, with similar results. Catholic parents protested readings from the Protestant Bible in Illinois public schools. School officials allowed students not wishing to take part in the exercise to leave the room, just as in the *Engel* case that was to follow more than fifty years later. The court banned the readings, finding "the exclusion of a pupil from this part of the school exercises in which the rest of the school joins, separates him from his fellows, puts him in a class by himself, deprives him of his equality with the other pupils, subjects him to a religious stigma and places him at a disadvantage in the school, which the law never contemplated."

Other courts, however, took the opposite stance, ruling that there were legitimate secular reasons for holding religious exercises. In Topeka, Kansas, in 1904, courts allowed a teacher to lead the class in reciting the Lord's Prayer every day. The teacher said the activity served only to quiet her class before their lessons.

An earlier case, decided by the Supreme Court of Massachusetts in 1866, ruled in favor of school officials who expelled a girl because she refused to bow her head during school prayers. The court agreed with the school that the exercise was meant only to ensure quiet and decorum.

CHRISTIAN AMENDMENT
Congress, too, became embroiled in the battle over the establishment clause. The Civil War and the unrest leading up to it led to the formation of the National Reform Association (NRA), a radical group of Christians who believed that the war was God's retribution on the nation. They were upset that the U.S. Constitution made no mention of God. As a remedy, they sought to add a fifteenth amendment to the Constitution in 1864 establishing the United States as a "Christian Nation." The so-called Christian Amendment would have changed the Preamble to the Constitution to read:

We, the people of the United States, humbly acknowledging Almighty God as the source of all authority and power in civil government, the Lord Jesus Christ as the Ruler among the nations, his revealed will as the supreme law of the land, in order to constitute a Christian government, . . .

AMENDING THE CONSTITUTION:
A LONG, HARD JOURNEY

In the more than two centuries since the U.S. Constitution was adopted, only twenty-seven amendments have been added to that historic document. The first ten amendments, called the Bill of Rights, were ratified, or approved, in 1791 as part of a compromise to win support for the original Constitution. They ensure individual rights.

Through the years Constitutional amendments have addressed a number of grievances and have righted wrongs. The Thirteenth Amendment abolished slavery in the United States. With the passage of the Fourteenth Amendment, the states had to abide by the rights guaranteed to citizens under the Bill of Rights. The Nineteenth Amendment, passed in 1920, allowed women to vote. In 1971, citizens ratified the Twenty-sixth Amendment, which gave eighteen-year-olds the right to vote.

Only once has an amendment been revoked. The Eighteenth Amendment, ratified in 1919, banned the manufacture, sale, and transportation of alcoholic liquors. The Twenty-first Amendment, which went into effect fourteen years later, repealed the alcohol ban.

The founders intentionally made it difficult to pass a constitutional amendment. The process involves a long, involved maze of hurdles that can take years to traverse. An amendment may be proposed in one of two ways:

1. Two-thirds of the state legislatures (thirty-three states in 2005) can convene a constitutional convention to propose an amendment, which must then be approved by three-fourths of the states. No amendment has yet been proposed by that route.
2. The second method is by joint resolution of Congress. Both the House of Representatives and

the Senate must approve the resolution by a two-thirds majority of members present. At least half the members of Congress must attend the session for the vote to count. Once Congress has approved the resolution, the amendment goes to the states for a vote.

Unlike regular bills, proposed amendments do not require the president's signature. Neither can a president veto an amendment. Three-fourths of the states (thirty-eight) must ratify the amendment for it to become part of the Constitution. A simple majority of a state's legislators must vote in favor of an amendment to ratify it. Alternately, a state may hold a constitutional convention at which a simple majority of the delegates is needed to ratify.

Every year citizens submit hundreds of proposed amendments to Congress. Most never get beyond a referral to a Congressional committee. Only a few are ever considered by the full House or Senate. Proposed amendments address a wide range of topics, from campaign spending to pornography to homelessness. Gay marriage, the Pledge of Allegiance's use of "under God," and school prayer have all been recent subjects of proposed amendments.

In 1918, Congress voted to allow states seven years in which to decide on ratification of the Eighteenth Amendment. That deadline has applied to most amendments since then. Several amendments proposed before that date but not enacted, and one since then, are technically still pending because Congress never issued a time limit for their ratification. Congress extended the deadline for passage of the Equal Rights Amendment by three years (until 1982) but the amendment failed to win ratification by three states.

The Twenty-seventh Amendment holds the record for the longest time between resolution and ratification. The amendment won final approval in 1992, 203 years after first being introduced. Originally proposed as part of the Bill of Rights, the amendment stipulates that Congressional pay raises cannot become effective until after the next election. Over the course of 215 years, Congress has submitted six amendments to the states that did not win approval. The six are as follows:

1. Article 1 of the Bill of Rights set out a formula to determine the number of representatives in the House (1789, still pending).
2. A proposed thirteenth amendment deprived Americans of their U.S. citizenship if they accepted, without Congress's consent, a title of nobility from a foreign government (1810, still pending).
3. Another proposed thirteenth amendment (the Corwin amendment) barred Congress from abolishing slavery (1861, still pending). President James Buchanan signed the amendment, the only one to be signed by a president.
4. The Child Labor Amendment gave Congress the power to "limit, regulate, and prohibit" labor by those under the age of eighteen (1924, still pending).
5. The Equal Rights Amendment guaranteed equal rights to men and women (1972, dead).
6. The District of Columbia Voting Rights Amendment granted Washington, D.C., residents full representation in Congress (1978, dead).

NRA members, among whom was U.S. Supreme Court Justice William Strong, circulated petitions supporting the measure among churches and Christian organizations throughout the country. Thousands of Americans signed these petitions, which were then sent to Congress.

Those who believed in the separation of church and state soon formed an organization of their own, the Free Religious Association (FRA), and adopted many of the same strategies to win support for their cause. They began circulating a counter-petition "asking Congress to preserve inviolate the great guarantees of religious liberty, and protesting against an amendment to the Constitution establishing religious tests."

On January 7, 1874, the FRA grabbed the attention of the nation by presenting to Congress a 953-foot-long petition signed by more than 35,000 people who opposed the Christian Amendment.

Undoubtedly impressed by the FRA petition and influenced by the Ohio Supreme Court decision in the Cincinnati case issued the year before, the House Judiciary Committee voted to table the proposal indefinitely. The committee reported that "it was inexpedient to put anything into the constitution or frame a government which might be construed to be a reference to any religious creed or doctrine." The members reminded Americans of "the dangers which the union between church and state had imposed upon so many nations of the Old World."

Government Aid and Religion

The spending of government money for students at religious schools also came under scrutiny by the public and the courts. Critics argued that the establishment clause barred such funding. Several court rulings narrowed the circumstances under which tax dollars could be spent on parochial students.

A 1930 case, *Cochran v. Louisiana State Board of Education*, involved the state's purchase of nonreligious textbooks for children in both public and parochial schools. Taxpayers objected to the use of their money to buy supplies for religious institutions. The U.S. Supreme Court allowed the expenditure, but the ruling made it clear that the funding was constitutional only because it benefited the students, not the religious school. The state also benefited, according to the Court, because its citizens were educated.

In another case, *Everson v. Board of Education*, decided in 1947, the Court laid down strict rules for government spending for religious school students. The case involved a New Jersey law that allowed local school boards to reimburse parents for the cost of busing students to school. The law applied to all students, whether they attended public or parochial schools. Arch Everson, a taxpayer in Ewing Township, sued the local school board when it enacted the policy. He claimed that using tax money to pay for transportation to and from parochial schools amounted to an establishment of religion.

In a five to four decision, the Supreme Court ruled against Everson, using much the same reasoning as in *Cochran*. The money, the Court noted, went to the parents, not the schools, and therefore met constitutional requirements. In his majority opinion, however, Justice Hugo Black set up strict limits on the government's involvement with religion. Even though the justices disagreed on the outcome of the case, they all agreed with Black's sweeping support for the separation of church and state under the establishment clause. The opinion was also significant because for the first time the Court asserted

that states as well as the federal government were banned
from aiding religion.

> Neither a state nor the Federal Government can
> set up a church. Neither can pass laws which aid
> one religion, aid all religions, or prefer one
> religion over another. Neither can force nor
> influence a person to go to or remain away from
> church against his will or force him to profess a
> belief or disbelief in any religion. No person can
> be punished for entertaining or professing
> religious beliefs or disbeliefs, for church
> attendance or non-attendance. No tax in any
> amount, large or small, can be levied to support
> any religious activities or institutions, whatever
> they may be called, or whatever form they may
> adopt to teach or practice religion.

Four of the justices dissented. They believed that the
Court should have ruled against state aid for parochial
schools for the very reasons Black outlined. "The
undertones of the opinion, advocating complete and
uncompromising separation of Church from State, seem
utterly discordant with its conclusion yielding support to
their commingling in educational matters," wrote
Justice Robert Jackson in a dissent joined by Justice
Felix Frankfurter. Justice Wiley B. Rutledge, who also
dissented, went even further in arguing against any type
of governmental connection with religion. The intent of
the First Amendment, Rutledge wrote, went beyond a
simple ban against a formal establishment of a state
church. Instead, the amendment's purpose "was to
create a complete and permanent separation of the
spheres of religious activity and civil authority by

comprehensively forbidding every form of public aid or support for religion."

The following year, the Court expanded *Everson*'s restrictions to include religious instruction in public schools. The case, *McCollum* v. *Board of Education*, began in 1945 in Champaign, Illinois. The local school board allowed private church groups to teach religion in the schools during regular school hours. Students could choose to attend Jewish, Protestant, or Roman Catholic classes held in their regular classrooms. Students who did not want to attend the weekly half-hour classes had to leave the classroom and study elsewhere.

Vashti McCollum chose not to allow her fifth-grade son, James, to attend the classes. She thought that offering such lessons in the schools violated the Constitution. During the religion classes, James was forced to sit in the hallway and read. Other students teased him. As the case made its way through the court system, attacks on the McCollum family escalated. James's classmates threatened him, vandals damaged the McCollum home, and Mrs. McCollum was fired from her job.

On March 9, 1948, the U.S. Supreme Court ruled that the lessons violated the Constitution's ban on government establishment of religion. The six to one landmark decision, again written by Justice Black, became the basis of many other rulings banning government involvement with religion. Going beyond his previous statements in *Everson*, Black made it clear that the Fourteenth Amendment's due process clause required states as well as the federal government to abide by the First Amendment's ban on the establishment of religion.

Justice Black wrote:

Pupils compelled by law to go to school for secular education are released in part from their legal duty upon the condition that they attend the religious classes. This is beyond all question a utilization of the tax-established and tax-supported public school system to aid religious groups to spread their faith. And it falls squarely under the ban of the First Amendment (made applicable to the States by the Fourteenth).

Concluding the opinion, Black emphasized that refusing to aid religious programs did not mean government was hostile to religion. He used Jefferson's analogy as he had in the previous case:

> To hold that a state cannot consistently with the First and Fourteenth Amendments utilize its public school system to aid any or all religious faiths or sects in the dissemination of their doctrines and ideals does not, as counsel urge, manifest a governmental hostility to religion or religious teachings. A manifestation of such hostility would be at war with our national tradition as embodied in the First Amendment's guaranty of the free exercise of religion. For the First Amendment rests upon the premise that both religion and government can best work to achieve their lofty aims if each is left free from the other within its respective sphere. Or, as we said in the *Everson* case, the First Amendment had erected a wall between Church and State which must be kept high and impregnable.

In a concurring opinion, Justice Frankfurter noted that students feel pressure to conform. Students would not want to set themselves apart from their peers by leaving the room, even if they did not agree with the lessons being taught in the religion classes. "The law of

FOURTEENTH AMENDMENT:
ENSURING RIGHTS FOR ALL

Section. 1. All persons born or naturalized in the United States and subject to the jurisdiction thereof, are citizens of the United States and of the State wherein they reside. No State shall make or enforce any law which shall abridge the privileges or immunities of citizens of the United States; nor shall any State deprive any person of life, liberty, or property, without due process of law; nor deny to any person within its jurisdiction the equal protection of the laws.

Section. 2. Representatives shall be apportioned among the several States according to their respective numbers, counting the whole number of persons in each State, excluding Indians not taxed. But when the right to vote at any election for the choice of electors for President and Vice President of the United States, Representatives in Congress, the Executive and Judicial officers of a State, or the members of the Legislature thereof, is denied to any of the male inhabitants of such State, being twenty-one years of age, and citizens of the United States, or in any way abridged, except for participation in rebellion, or other crime, the basis of representation therein shall be reduced in the proportion which the number of such male citizens shall bear to the whole number of male citizens twenty-one years of age in such State.

Section. 3. No person shall be a Senator or Representative in Congress, or elector of President and Vice President, or hold any office, civil or military, under the United States, or under any State, who, having previously taken an oath, as a member of Congress, or as an officer of the United States, or as a member of any State legislature, or as an executive or judicial officer of any State, to support the Constitution of the United States, shall have engaged in insurrection or rebellion against the same, or given aid or comfort to the enemies thereof. But Congress may by a vote of two-thirds of each House, remove such disability.

Section. 4. The validity of the public debt of the United States, authorized by law, including debts incurred for payment of pensions and bounties for services in suppressing insurrection or rebellion, shall not be questioned. But neither the United States nor any State shall assume or pay any debt or obligation incurred in aid of insurrection or rebellion against the United States, or any claim for the loss or emancipation of any slave; but all such debts, obligations and claims shall be held illegal and void.

Section. 5. The Congress shall have power to enforce, by appropriate legislation, the provisions of this article.

The First Amendment bars Congress from making any law that would establish a particular religion or prevent Americans from freely exercising their religion. It says nothing about what states can and cannot do.

For years the states used that loophole to pass laws that conflicted with the First Amendment's protections. In the 1845 case *Permoli* v. *Municipality No. 1 of City of New Orleans*, for example, the Supreme Court upheld the states' argument that the First Amendment did not apply to them. Justice John Catron, writing for the majority, ruled: "The Constitution makes no provision for protecting the citizens of the respective states in their religious liberties; this is left to the state constitutions and laws."

After the Civil War, Congress sought to close that particular loophole with the passage of the Fourteenth Amendment. Whites in the South had used the loophole to deprive freed slaves of their rights as citizens. With the ratification of the amendment on July 28, 1868, former slaves and all others "born or naturalized in the United States" automatically became American citizens. As citizens they could vote, own property, and engage in business

The amendment also directed the states not to deprive anyone, citizen and noncitizen alike, of "life liberty, or property, without due process of law;" nor the "equal protection of the laws." In addition, the amendment specifically forbade the states from limiting citizens' "privileges or immunities."

For decades after the amendment was passed, however, it offered little protection against state actions. The Slaughterhouse cases in 1873 set the stage for a conservative view of the amendment. The Court, in those cases, ruled against the plaintiffs, who complained that the state by its actions had deprived them of their rights as citizens guaranteed under the Fourteenth Amendment. The ruling allowed states to control the civil rights of their citizens.

Over time, however, the Court began to apply the Fourteenth Amendment to protect citizens against wrongful actions by the states. Under this doctrine, the rights listed in the Bill of Rights are said to be incorporated by the Fourteenth Amendment. This doctrine has been referred to as "the second Bill of Rights" because it protected against unreasonable state power as the original ten amendments protected against federal abuses. Among other things, the policy played a key role in preserving Americans' religious liberties against state laws that favored certain religions.

One of the earliest cases in which the Court used the incorporation doctrine to limit a state's power was Gitlow v. New York. The case involved a socialist named Benjamin Gitlow, who was arrested after distributing copies of a paper urging people to strike and to take "revolutionary mass action." The state convicted Gitlow of advocating the overthrow of the government. In its decision, issued in 1925, the Court ruled against Gitlow because his actions endangered the state. Nevertheless, the Court asserted that the Fourteenth Amendment required states as well as Congress not to abridge the First Amendment's guarantee of free speech:

> We may and do assume that freedom of speech and of the press—which are protected by the First Amendment from abridgment by Congress—are among the fundamental personal rights and "liberties" protected by the due process clause of the Fourteenth Amendment from impairment by the States.

In their dissent, Justices Oliver Wendell Holmes and Louis Brandeis argued that Gitlow's diatribe presented no immediate danger to the government and should be protected under the Constitution's free speech guarantees. They, too, supported the doctrine that the Fourteenth Amendment protected free speech from state control.

During the 1930s and 1940s, the Supreme Court applied other First Amendment rights to the states. The Warren Court in the 1950s and 1960s made extensive use of the incorporation doctrine. With its focus on civil and individual rights, the Warren Court used the doctrine to order school desegregation, ban school prayers, and establish protections for criminal defendants. Later Courts have used the doctrine to strike down state laws banning abortion, guarantee privacy rights, and ensure other rights not specifically mentioned in the Constitution.

imitation operates," Frankfurter wrote, joined in his opinion by three other justices, "and nonconformity is not an outstanding characteristic of children. The result is an obvious pressure upon children to attend."

Many schools throughout the country had similar "release time" programs, as they were called. In the wake of *McCollum*, school boards attempted to avoid lawsuits by using various tactics. New York City formulated a plan similar to the Champaign policy. Classes were held during school hours but not on school property. Students attending the classes left the school premises. Those not participating went to a study hall at the school. Teachers kept track of both sets of students, and classes were suspended during the religious lessons.

This policy was also challenged. The case came before the U.S. Supreme Court in 1952 as *Zorach* v. *Clauson*. This time, a majority of the justices found the plan acceptable. The New York program involved no expenditure of taxpayers' money. Children not attending religion classes were neither pressured nor ostracized. With that in mind, the majority found no reason why the government should not accommodate the churches.

Writing the opinion for the Court, Justice Douglas acknowledged the religious heritage of Americans: "We are a religious people whose institutions presuppose a Supreme Being." If the New York law were found unconstitutional, he said, students could not be excused even for religious holidays. Rather than severing all ties between state and church, Douglas said, the Constitution allows the state to cooperate with religious authorities. Such cooperation, he added, "follows the best of our tradition." He explained:

> For [government] then respects the religious nature of our people and accommodates the public

service to their spiritual needs. To hold that it may not would be to find in the Constitution a requirement that the government show a callous indifference to religious groups. That would be preferring those who believe in no religion over those who do believe.

Douglas's reasoning, however, did not persuade the three dissenting justices. Justice Black voiced alarm over the use of the public schools to channel students into religious classes. Such assistance, he noted, "injects political and party prejudices into a holy field. It too often substitutes force for prayer, hate for love, and persecution for persuasion." He warned that "government should not be allowed, under cover of the soft euphemism of 'co-operation', to steal into the sacred area of religious choice."

Justice Jackson, in a separate dissent, argued that the school "serves as a temporary jail for a pupil who will not go to Church." He added, "The day that this country ceases to be free for irreligion it will cease to be free for religion—except for that sect that can win political power."

As the decade wore on, school boards, public officials, and courts increasingly addressed conflicts over the relationship between religion and government. Clearly, it was an issue that would not be settled by one case or two. By the time *Engel* v. *Vitale* reached the Supreme Court in 1962, it became apparent that the justices would use the case to cover new ground in the battle over the separation of church and state.

four
A Prayer Goes to Court

when the Herricks School Board received notice that the Long Island parents in the *Engel* case had filed a petition to remove the Regents' Prayer from New York schools, the board members voted to oppose the effort. Bertram Daiker, the board's attorney, would lead the fight. Daiker had represented the board on various issues and had experience in appeals cases.

The parents entrusted their case to ACLU attorney William Butler. A noted human rights lawyer, Butler had served as staff counsel to the ACLU and was a member of the board of the New York Civil Liberties Union, the local ACLU chapter. He had been prominent in the battle to protect the rights of citizens threatened during the "Red Scare" of the 1950s when Congress was intent on exposing supposed Communists and "fellow travelers"—those who merely sympathized with the Communists' goals.

Butler later recalled why he was chosen for the school prayer case: "When the case came up, they decided that the lawyer . . . must be Catholic, that is, someone taking the attitude that he is DEFENDING prayer and religious freedom, not attacking it. And they looked down at the end of the table and saw a nice Irish-Catholic boy—William Butler." Stanley Geller, also an ACLU lawyer, assisted Butler in the case.

Another group of sixteen parents, led by Henry

Hollenberg, supported prayer in the schools. They hired Porter Chandler, an attorney who had represented Catholic organizations in a number of cases, to present their views in court. The group of parents included Jews, Protestants, and Catholics as well as one woman who was not a member of any church. Among them, they had thirty-seven children in the New York public schools.

The case soon drew national attention. The five families opposing the prayer received angry letters denouncing their stand. Anonymous telephone callers spewed threats against them and their children. One of the mothers told a reporter she no longer allowed her children to answer the telephone because of the abusive calls.

Despite the fear of violence, the five parents pushed on. In their petition to the New York Supreme Court in January 1959, the parents argued that the school board's order to include the prayer in school exercises violated the establishment clause of the First Amendment. The court turned down their request for a jury trial. Instead, Judge Bernard Meyer, presiding at Nassau County Court House, reviewed the case. He studied the written arguments, or briefs, submitted by the case's three lawyers.

Months went by as the judge considered the grave constitutional questions involved. Finally, Judge Meyer issued his lengthy ruling. The establishment clause of the First Amendment, Meyer ruled, did not ban the prayer as long as the schools did not require students to participate. Supporting the school board's claims, Meyer ruled that the Regents' Prayer was not "religious instruction," did not represent the beliefs of any particular religion, and did not show preference to certain religious groups. He also ruled that there was no "indirect compulsion" of students to say the prayer. "Freedom of religion," the judge added, "includes the right publicly to express religious beliefs."

However, the judge warned the school board to "take

affirmative steps to protect the rights of those who, for whatever reason, choose not to participate." He ordered the board to set up policies to ensure that students not be compelled to recite the prayer. The court postponed a final decision on the parents' petition until such policies had been adopted.

"The religion clauses [in the First Amendment] protect non-believers as well as believers," Meyer wrote; "every individual has a constitutional right personally to be free from religion, but he may not compel others to adopt the same attitude."

A First Step

The judge's decision disappointed Lawrence Roth. "It seemed strange to me that a judge would render a decision saying . . . 'this prayer is legal but if you do so and so it's going to be even more legal,'" he said.

Butler, however, saw the loss as the first step to a much larger victory that would have national impact. If the school board had lost, the board members might have abandoned the fight because of the cost of appealing a ruling to the next higher court. The ACLU, with its national funding, was prepared to appeal the case all the way to the U.S. Supreme Court. As the losing party, the parents' group could force the school board back into court.

Butler said later that he was "scared that we might win in the lower courts. That way we would not have had a national decision. One way to cut the bridges of a civil libertarian quickly is to render a decision in the lower court."

Even before the school board could act on the judge's order, Butler appealed the case to the Appellate Division of the New York Supreme Court. The court again ruled in favor of the school board, basing its decision on Judge Meyer's opinion.

Responding to the court order, the school board, on

September 3, 1959, passed a set of rules regarding the morning ritual. They stipulated that:

1. School officials could not urge students in any way to participate in the prayer.
2. Students who did not want to say the prayer could be excused and leave the room during the ritual if they wished.
3. Parents could request that their children be excused from reciting the prayer by writing to the school principal.

After implementing the new policy, the school board asked the court to dismiss the parents' petition. The court granted the request. Unfazed, Butler took the case to the next level, the New York Court of Appeals, the state's highest court.

On July 7, 1961, the appeals court, in a five to two vote, upheld the lower court's decision and ruled that New York students could continue to say the Regents' Prayer.

The outcome reflected the complexity of the case. The judges wrote three separate opinions supporting the prayer, none of which received the vote of a majority of the court. Two judges dissented. Chief Judge Charles S. Desmond wrote in favor of the prayer: "That the First Amendment was ever intended to forbid as an 'establishment of religion' a simple declaration of belief in God is so contrary to history as to be impossible of acceptance."

In voting for the school board, the judges based their decision on four factors argued by Daiker:

1. The prayer was nonsectarian and did not favor a particular religion.
2. The prayer was voluntary.

3. Prayers had been said at public schools for many years.
4. Americans are a religious people. The founders never intended to require actions "hostile" to religion—such as banning prayer in public schools.

The dissent, however, encouraged Butler. Signed by two judges, the minority opinion stated that the Regents' Prayer "cannot help but lead to a gradual erosion of the mighty bulwark erected by the First Amendment," and therefore was unconstitutional. The opinion bolstered Butler's own arguments.

While Butler saw the delays as just part of court procedure, the five families involved in the case found the waiting difficult. Daniel Roth later recalled that teachers resented him and his brother more than the students did. "I definitely remember an antagonism from the teachers, no question about that," he said later. "There were comments made. I remember an eighth-grade teacher in particular. She would make snide remarks about what my father was doing. . . . I was certainly singled out by her for humiliation."

Even so, the families agreed that Butler should take the next step: an appeal to the U.S. Supreme Court.

PETITIONING THE SUPREME COURT
The U.S. Supreme Court hears only a small portion of the thousands of cases submitted for review each year. In 1960, the Court considered 2,313 requests for a hearing. That number has increased rapidly. In 2004, the Court had more than nine thousand cases on the docket. The justices hear oral arguments in only about one hundred cases per term.

To be accepted for review by the Supreme Court, cases must deal with one or more of three issues: constitutional rights or questions, conflicts between rulings of different courts, or rulings by a state court on a federal law.

Through the Court System

First Stop: State Court

Almost all cases (about 95 percent) start in state courts. These courts go by various names, depending on the state in which they operate: circuit, district, municipal, county, or superior courts. The case is tried and decided by a judge, a panel of judges, or a jury.

The side that loses can then appeal to the next level.

First Stop: Federal Court

U.S. DISTRICT COURT—About 5 percent of cases begin their journey in federal court. Most of these cases concern federal laws, the U.S. Constitution, or disputes that involve two or more states. They are heard in one of the ninety-four U.S. district courts in the nation.

U.S. COURT OF INTERNATIONAL TRADE—Federal court cases involving international trade appear in the U.S. Court of International Trade.

U.S. CLAIMS COURT—The U.S. Claims Court hears federal cases that involve more than $10,000, Indian claims, and some disputes with government contractors.

The loser in federal court can appeal to the next level.

Appeals: State Cases

Forty states have appeals courts that hear cases that have come from the state courts. In states without an appeals court, the case goes directly to the state supreme court.

Appeals: Federal Cases

U.S. CIRCUIT COURT—Cases appealed from U.S. district courts go to U.S. circuit courts of appeals. There are twelve circuit courts that handle cases from throughout the nation. Each district court and every state and territory are assigned to one of the twelve circuits. Appeals in a few state cases—those that deal with rights guaranteed by the U.S. Constitution—are also heard in this court.

U.S. COURT OF APPEALS—Cases appealed from the U.S. Court of International Trade and the U.S. Claims Court are heard by the U.S. Court of Appeals for the Federal Circuit. Among the cases heard in this court are those involving patents and minor claims against the federal government.

FurTHer APPeaLs: sTaTe supreme courT

Cases appealed from state appeals courts go to the highest courts in the state—usually called supreme court. In New York, the state's highest court is called the court of appeals. Most state cases do not go beyond this point.

FInaL APPeaLs: u.s. supreme courT

The U.S. Supreme Court is the highest court in the country. Its decision on a case is the final word. The Court decides issues that can affect every person in the nation. It has decided cases on slavery, abortion, school segregation, and many other important issues.

The Court selects the cases it will hear—usually around one hundred each year. Four of the nine justices must vote to consider a case in order for it to be heard. Almost all cases have been appealed from the lower courts (either state or federal).

Most people seeking a decision from the Court submit a petition for certiorari. Certiorari means that the case will be moved from a lower court to a higher court for review. The Court receives about seven thousand of these requests annually. The petition outlines the case and gives reasons why the Court should review it.

In rare cases, for example *New York Times* v. *United States*, an issue must be decided immediately. When such a case is of national importance, the Court allows it to bypass the usual lower court system and hears the case directly.

To win a spot on the Court's docket, a case must fall within one of the following categories:

- Disputes between states and the federal government or between two or more states. The Court also reviews cases involving ambassadors, consuls, and foreign ministers.
- Appeals from state courts that haves ruled on a federal question.
- Appeals from federal appeals courts (about two-thirds of all requests fall into this category).

Usually lawyers file a petition with the Court asking that their case be heard and outlining the reasons the Court should consider it. This is called a petition for certiorari. *Certiorari* comes from the Latin word meaning "to be more fully informed." If the Court grants certiorari, the records of the case are transferred from the lower courts to allow the justices to be fully informed of the proceedings. No witnesses testify at the hearings, and there is no jury.

The Court term begins on the first Monday in October and ends in June or July, depending on the caseload. The chief justice reviews the cases and chooses the ones that

THE MEMBERS OF THE U.S. SUPREME COURT IN 1953. FRONT ROW, FROM LEFT: JUSTICES FELIX FRANKFURTER, HUGO L. BLACK, CHIEF JUSTICE EARL WARREN, STANLEY F. REED, AND WILLIAM O. DOUGLAS. BACK ROW, FROM LEFT: JUSTICES TOM C. CLARK, ROBERT H. JACKSON, HAROLD H. BURTON, AND SHERMAN MINTON.

Related cases

While the two sides prepared their case, a federal district court decision in Pennsylvania offered support for Butler's arguments. In 1959, Edward Schempp had sued to prevent the Abington Township School Board from requiring Bible reading in school. Schempp was a Unitarian with two children in high school. The Bible reading contradicted his religious convictions.

The court decided in Schempp's favor. The decision in *Schempp* v. *School District of Abington Township* outlawed the reading of Bible verses at public schools in Pennsylvania. The ruling nullified a Pennsylvania law, passed in 1949, that required the reading of ten or more Bible verses at the start of every school day.

Abington High School broadcast the readings, from a King James version of the Bible, over the school's public address system. The school allowed students to follow along using a Catholic or Jewish version of the Bible if they wanted to. The reading contained no commentary or interpretation of the Bible verses. Following the broadcast, the reader led students in reciting the Lord's Prayer and the Pledge of Allegiance. All were expected to participate in the morning exercises.

After the 1959 court decision, the Pennsylvania legislature amended the law. Students who chose not to participate could leave the room during the morning ritual. Schempp sued again. He believed the new law would set his children apart and damage their relationships with both students and teachers.

On February 1, 1962, the federal court ruled that the amended version of the act also violated the Constitution. Chief Judge John Biggs Jr. wrote, "The fact that some pupils, or theoretically all pupils, might be excused from attendance at the exercise does not mitigate the obligatory nature of the ceremony. . . . Since the statute required the reading of the 'Holy Bible,' a Christian document, the practice . . . prefers the Christian religion."

Such a finding by a federal court would bolster Butler's case. A similar case, involving the Pledge of Allegiance, threatened to weaken Butler's position. That case had also been brought to court in New York by a group of parents whose children attended public schools in that state. These parents objected to the words "under God" in the pledge and believed their addition by Congress in 1954 violated the First Amendment's guarantee of religious liberty. They asked the court to order the Commissioner of Education of New York to delete the words from the pledge recited by the state's schoolchildren. The parents used much the same arguments Butler had pursued in *Engel* v. *Vitale*. The lower court turned them down, and their appeal was pending in the Court of Appeals in New York when *Engel* reached the Supreme Court. The Pledge of Allegiance case would eventually be dismissed, but the issue regularly reappeared in the nation's courts.

From the start, Butler had tried to separate the Regents' Prayer from the Pledge of Allegiance. He did not want to dilute his case by linking it to one that he believed did not apply. Lawyers for the school board repeatedly tried to equate the prayer with the pledge. Butler argued that the prayer was undeniably a religious ritual that aimed to persuade children of the power and glory of God. Reciting the pledge, however, was a political, not a religious, act, he said. Its purpose was not to teach religion, but to instill patriotism.

FIVE
BEFORE THE SUPREME COURT

FOR THE LAWYERS INVOLVED in the *Engel* case, Tuesday, April 3, 1962, was a day they would remember for a lifetime. On that day, each took his turn to stand before America's most powerful justices and answer questions and present arguments that he hoped would win the case for his side. The lawyers had one-half hour each to make their case. William J. Butler, representing the five parents opposed to the prayer, would go first, followed by Bertram B. Daiker, speaking for the school board. Porter R. Chandler, lawyer for the parents supporting the prayer, would end the session.

Chandler had argued successfully before the Court in a 1936 case, *Valentine* v. *United States*, involving the extradition of American citizens to France. He had also filed an *amicus curiae* brief for the New York State Catholic Welfare Committee in a 1952 Supreme Court case about film censorship.

Butler, too, had filed a brief, for the ACLU, in a previous U.S. Supreme Court case in 1958, although he had never argued before the Court.

Daiker had never had any dealings with the Supreme Court. The forty-seven-year-old lawyer had been handling cases for twenty years when the *Engel* suit brought him to Washington, D.C. In addition to the school board, he represented a group of Lutheran churches among other clients and had argued many appeals in the lower courts. Years later, Daiker still remembered the awe-inspiring proceeding. "It is an intimidating experience no matter how long you've been practicing law," he recalled during an interview in 2004. The "very austere surroundings" of the court room, with its twenty-four columns of Italian marble and forty-four-foot-high ceiling, could make even the most self-assured lawyer feel insignificant.

Even so, Daiker entered the courtroom with the assurance that two other courts had agreed with him in the case. "I had an 11 to 2 box score," he recalled. "Only two [lower court] judges thought I was wrong."

That morning he would try for yet another win.

"GOD save THIS Honorable court"
Shortly after 10 a.m. the Court marshal announced the entrance of the seven justices who would hear the case. In a booming voice, he called out the words that had opened Court hearings since the first session in 1790:

> The Honorable, the Chief Justice and the Associate Justices of the Supreme Court of the United States. Oyez! Oyez! Oyez! All persons having business before the Honorable, the Supreme Court of the United States, are admonished to draw near and give their attention, for the Court is now sitting. God save the United States and this Honorable Court!

Oyez, the traditional proclamation used to signify the opening of court proceedings for centuries, originates from a Middle English word meaning "hear ye." The marshal repeated the word three times, followed by the rest of the proclamation, including the usual plea to

God, as the black-robed justices emerged from behind red velvet drapes to take their seats at the raised, polished mahogany bench. They sat in order of seniority, Chief Justice Earl Warren at the center with the most senior justice, Hugo L. Black, at his right, and the next longest-serving justice, Felix Frankfurter, at his left. The remaining justices alternated between right and left, in order of their years of service: William O. Douglas, Thomas C. Clark, John M. Harlan, William J. Brennan Jr., and Potter Stewart.

An eight-member Court would hear the case, but only seven members would ultimately decide the outcome. President John F. Kennedy had recently appointed Byron White to replace Charles Whitaker on the Court. White, approved by the Senate, had not yet been sworn in as a Supreme Court justice. He would take his oath of office on April 16, too late to participate in the *Engel* case. Although Justice Frankfurter listened to the oral arguments, he would not vote on the case. On April 5, two days after the arguments had been heard, Frankfurter collapsed at his desk and was rushed to the hospital. After a lengthy leave of absence, the seventy-nine-year-old justice, the victim of a stroke, resigned from the Court in August of that year.

News reporters crowded into the courtroom to hear arguments in the landmark case. News media around the nation had followed the case as it worked its way through the court system.

Guardians of Freedom

Scores of outraged citizens had written to the Supreme Court, urging the justices to allow schoolchildren to say prayers in school. The justices never saw the letters. Aides handled the correspondence.

Supreme Court justices are called on to decide cases based on law and reasoned argument. The U.S.

Constitution, not public opinion, serves as their guide. Unlike the political leaders in Congress and the White House who depend on voter support to keep their posts, Supreme Court justices are appointed for life. Citizens and lobbyists may apply political pressure on elected officials during the nomination and approval of particular justices. Once justices have been appointed to the bench, however, they can be forced from office only through impeachment and conviction. In the more than two centuries since the Supreme Court first assembled, only one justice, Samuel Chase, has been impeached, in 1805, and the Senate failed to convict him.

Although freed from the insecurities of office felt by elected officials, justices remain connected to the political life of the nation. Many justices have had highly successful political careers and continue to keep an eye on the political mood of the country. Often justices tailor decisions or time their release with politics in mind. Earl Warren's Court chose not to require the South to desegregate its schools immediately, in part because the states lacked the political will to do so. The Court delayed the announcement of the abortion case decision, *Roe* v. *Wade*, until after President Richard Nixon's inauguration in 1973, presumably to avoid embarrassing the anti-choice president. Justice Abe Fortas resigned from the Court in 1969 under intense political pressure after questions arose over a fee he had accepted from a private foundation.

Justices' opinions often reflect certain political views. One group of justices may take a conservative stand, while another group may vote as a liberal or moderate bloc. But justices can and do change their views while on the Court. This can frustrate those who supported their appointment. Earl Warren was a Republican with conservative views on crime and other social issues when he was appointed chief justice by President Dwight Eisenhower. Eisenhower later called Warren's nomination "the biggest damn-fool mistake I ever made" after the Warren Court issued several landmark decisions on school desegregation, the right of accused criminals not to incriminate themselves, and other issues.

Supreme Court justices often reflect the views of their time. In the *Dred Scott* case, the Court upheld slavery and ruled that no black man or woman could be a citizen of the United States. Another Court decision, in *Plessy* v. *Ferguson*, ruled that enforced segregation by race was constitutional. Both cases were eventually overturned by succeeding Courts.

Other Supreme Court decisions have challenged the status quo in upholding the rights of Americans. *Brown* v. *Board of Education*, the landmark 1954 case that made school segregation illegal, disrupted a way of life that had existed for half the country when it ordered equal access to education for African Americans.

But the Court, more often than not, upholds previous decisions. It can take decades for the Court to overturn even the most deplorable decisions. For example, the Court's 1896 *Plessy* v. *Ferguson* decision was the law of the land for

U.S. CHIEF JUSTICE EARL WARREN IN HIS WASHINGTON, D.C., OFFICE IN MARCH 1961. A YEAR LATER, WARREN WOULD LEAD THE COURT THAT STRUCK DOWN SCHOOL PRAYER IN THE *ENGEL* CASE.

fifty-eight years until the Warren Court overturned it in *Brown* v. *Board of Education*. Sometimes the nation itself takes action against a bad decision, as in the *Dred Scott* case. That opinion remained intact until the passage of the Thirteenth, Fourteenth, and Fifteenth amendments to the Constitution.

As the highest court in the land, the Supreme Court has the power to override laws and actions of both Congress and the president. It is that authority—the power of judicial review—that has allowed the Court to defend the rights of minorities, to protect civil liberties, and to promote political equality. When the Court takes such action to preserve the Constitution and its guarantees for all citizens, it stands as a guardian of American freedom against the pressures of majority rule.

Butler's Case

The players in the *Engel* case waited in the hushed courtroom to present their arguments. Hanging high above the justices' bench, a large, round clock ticked away the minutes. A light stood ready to signal red when the speaker had used his allotted time.

At Warren's invitation, Butler gathered his papers, rose, and walked to the lectern before the justices. After addressing the Court, the lawyer asserted that the case involved "an attempt by the State to introduce religious education and observances into the public school system of our Nation." He quoted the Regents' reasons for having schoolchildren recite the prayer: to protect "the peace and safety of our country and our State" by "teaching our children . . . that Almighty God is their creator." Butler continued with his reading of the Regents' record:

> We believe that thus the school will fulfill its high
> function of supplementing the training of the

84

WILLIAM BUTLER, THE ACLU LAWYER WHO ARGUED THE CASE FOR THE PARENTS OPPOSED TO SCHOOL PRAYER IN *ENGEL* v. *VITALE*.

home, ever intensifying in the child that love for God, for parents, and for home which is the mark of true character, training, and a sure guarantee of a country's welfare.

Under questioning from the justices, Butler acknowledged that the Board of Regents had recommended, not required, that the prayer be said by local schools. "It was left to the local school boards to adopt or not to adopt," he noted. The Herricks school board, he added, was one of a number of school systems to adopt the prayer. At first, he said, the Herricks schools required each student to recite the prayer in unison at the start of the school day. After the lower court forbade a mandatory prayer, the school board made the prayer a voluntary activity. Children who objected, Butler said, could leave the room if their parents wrote a letter asking that they be excused. Since the adoption of the new policy, Butler told the Court, he knew of no parent who had written such a request to the school and no child who had been excused. Only one request—that the child stay in the room but remain silent during the prayer—had been made, Butler said.

Butler argued that reciting the prayer in class violated both the establishment clause and the free exercise section of the First Amendment. Because little children do not usually like to be thought of as different, even a voluntary prayer could be seen as coercive, he said. He noted that he planned to use Justice Frankfurter's "brilliant dissertation" in the *McCollum* case (barring religious teaching in public schools) to bolster his arguments.

"As far as I'm concerned, you may assume I remember it," Frankfurter responded to general laughter from those in the courtroom.

Butler continued. He noted that the facts of the case were similar to those in *McCollum*: The religious activity in both occurred during school hours, on school property, with the cooperation of state officials. In both cases, the activity was voluntary. In addition, the prayer case involved the participation of teachers, which Butler contended made his case even stronger than *McCollum*.

In response to questions from the justices, Butler said that both sides agreed that the purpose of the Regents' Prayer was to teach religion in the public schools. "There's no question whether or not this religious activity is designed to bring the children into a religious activity which in the long run [according to the opposing briefs], will preserve the religious and even Christian heritage of our society."

Justice Harlan asked, "Is that a bad thing?"

Butler took the opportunity to proclaim the main purpose of his clients' case—not to destroy religion but to protect it.

> I want to make it absolutely clear before this Court that I come here not as an antagonist of religion, that my clients are deeply religious people; that we come here in the firm belief that the best safety of religion in the United States, and freedom of religion, is to keep religion out of our public life and not to confound . . . the civil with the religious.

The parents Butler represented were not against prayer, not against God, not against religion. The issue, Butler noted, was the fact that the government had created and recommended a prayer for public schoolchildren. This, he contended, clearly violated the First Amendment's prohibition against establishing a religion. "It's the beginning of the end of religious freedom," Butler said, "when religious activity such as this is incorporated into the public school system of the United States."

In response to further questions from the justices, Butler said he believed the Constitution barred schools from reading prayers or passages from any book linked to a religion (including the Christian Bible and the

Muslim Qu'ran) when the goal was to encourage children to embrace certain beliefs. "Of course," he said, "I distinguish between teaching religion and teaching about religion . . . all subjects should be free to be taught in the public schools. But when [the public school] engages in religious activity, where the avowed purpose is to promote religion, one religion, all religions, then I think this is barred . . . by the First Amendment." Butler said he saw no constitutional problem in having schoolchildren observe a five-minute period of silence for meditation.

Justice Douglas followed with a recitation of the opening words of the Court: "God save the United States and this honorable Court." The Board of Regents' brief had cited the customary words of the Court crier as proof that religious references were acceptable in government affairs. "We haven't decided whether that's constitutional or not, have we?" Douglas asked. "We have not decided whether compulsory prayer in the halls of Congress is constitutional. Is that case on its way here?"

Butler replied, "If it is, Your Honor, I'm glad I'm not bringing it." That brought more laughter from the audience.

Butler noted that James Madison had believed the use of chaplains in the Senate and the House was unconstitutional. But he quickly turned from that issue to the one at hand. A prayer in school differed from references to God at court, on coins, or in other instances, he said. For one thing, Butler said, every child was required by law to attend school. Secondly, teachers and government officials were teaching children the prayer.

This led to Butler's argument that the prayer also violated the free exercise clause. Even though the school board stipulated that the prayer was voluntary, children felt coerced to say it in order to fit in, Butler said. This

88

social pressure, he contended, interfered with the children's right to freely practice their religion.

Butler noted that it would be difficult for a child to leave the room during the prayer, even if the child and the parents objected to the ritual. Leaving would focus the entire class's attention on the child, Butler said. "They'd have to stop after the salute to the flag, send the child out of the room somewhere, and then, after the prayer was said, have somebody go out and tell the child to come back in."

He added: "Little children want to be with other little children." Few parents, he said, would want to brand their children as outcasts by requiring them to leave an activity in which all of the other children willingly participated.

"Isn't this really compulsion?" Butler asked the Court. "Would the little child . . . leave the classroom; or would the parent be expected to ask the school system to excuse his child, who may be singled out as a nonconformist?" Frankfurter had used such an argument in the decision in the *McCollum* case, as Butler had already noted.

Butler compared children who had to leave the room because of their religion to those who were segregated by race before the Supreme Court made such action illegal. Like black children, these children, too, Butler said, might suffer from "an indelible mark on [their] mind" from such treatment.

Next Butler argued against four points raised in the opposing briefs. The school board lawyers had cited the *Zorach* ruling in contending that the regents were accommodating religion and preserving the nation's religious heritage by recommending the prayer. Butler noted that unlike the religious instruction allowed by the *Zorach* ruling, the Regents' Prayer took place inside the school building, was created by state officials, and was led by the state's teachers. While the government can sometimes cooperate with religion, Butler said, it cannot "condone a religious activity where the State itself composes its own prayer, and then it's instituted in a compulsory institution."

On the second point, Butler disputed his opponent's comparison to the Pledge of Allegiance. The school board's brief had argued that the schools followed the requirements laid down by the *Barnette* case. Therefore, the lawyers argued, the prayer, like the pledge, could be recited as long as students were not forced to participate. Butler quoted Justice Frankfurter in his rebuttal: "One [the pledge] is the act of allegiance of political faith and the other [the Regents' Prayer] is an act of religion." He argued that the first was not barred by the Constitution, while the second was. Even though the words "under God" had been inserted into the pledge by Congress in 1954, Butler contended the purpose of the pledge itself was political rather than religious.

Butler then addressed the issue of majority rule. "The very purpose of the Constitution," he told the Court, "is to protect the minority against the majority, to protect the weak against the strong in matters of keeping separate forever the functions of the civil and the religious."

Finally, Butler reiterated that his clients were not out to destroy religion but to preserve religious liberty. While noting that four of his five clients were deeply religious, he noted that the rights of nonbelievers were as important as those of believers. "The State can no more prefer one religion as against another than it can compel one to believe or not to believe."

Under intense questioning from Justice Brennan, Butler argued that even if all the parents agreed with the content of the prayer, having children recite it in a public school would still violate the First Amendment. That would be true, Butler said, even if the prayer itself contained the same words as the Supreme Court opening proclamation, "God save the United States and this school." It would still be a religious ritual, he contended, "a religious activity, which is barred by the First Amendment."

Butler ended his defense with an answer to a question posed by Justice Frankfurter. Public schools, said Butler, are secular institutions, and rightly so. "The public school system," he told the Court, "can never be used by the State for religious purposes." The founders of our nation, he added, established such a system "in an attempt to protect religious freedom, in the long run, of us all."

With that, Butler said his thanks and sat down.

Daiker's views

Chief Justice Warren invited Bertram Daiker to make his case before the Court. Daiker, speaking for the school board, and Porter Chandler, representing the larger group of parents, would divide their time in speaking for the inclusion of the prayer in the New York schools' morning rituals.

Daiker began, as Butler had, by reading the words of the prayer to the Court. Disputing Butler's claim that the prayer involved the teaching of religion, Daiker argued that the words merely reflected American tradition and heritage. The nation's historic documents—from the Mayflower Compact to the Declaration of Independence to the constitutions of forty-nine of fifty states—all recognized "the existence of an almighty God, a Supreme Being," Daiker said. He pointed out that nineteen states in addition to New York had filed briefs with the Court supporting the regents' position.

In previous rulings, the lawyer argued, the Court had said that "the state and religion need not be hostile to each other." The First Amendment's ban on a state religion applied to the Herricks School District as it did to every other public entity, Daiker acknowledged. But, he argued, that did not mean there could be no religious state. "This Court has said many times we are essentially a religious people," Daiker noted.

The Court itself began proceedings with a traditional plea for God's blessings, Daiker said. President John F. Kennedy had used similar words at the end of his message to the American people earlier that year. Was mention of a Supreme Being on a public occasion the same as the establishment of religion, Daiker asked the Court. In his view, it was not.

Chief Justice Warren asked if Daiker would feel differently if the Court required all lawyers to recite the Regents' Prayer before presenting their cases. Such a requirement—a religious test for public office—would be unconstitutional, Daiker replied.

He further acknowledged that if public schools *required* students to say the prayer—even though it merely expressed an American tradition and was not objectionable—it would be unconstitutional. But, Daiker noted, the school board in this case did not require students to say the prayer.

"The prayer here as such is not unconstitutional. But if it is administered with compulsion, then we have an unconstitutional practice," he told the Court. The school board took that into consideration, he said, when it made the prayer voluntary. The original order by the school board merely instructed principals to have classes recite the prayer after the salute to the flag. Daiker added that principals and teachers were told not to require students to say the prayer.

Justice Black asked if Daiker considered the prayer to be an avowal of religious faith. "Yes," the lawyer replied.

The justice then asked him why the Board of Regents had issued the prayer. According to Daiker, the regents wanted to promote "the belief in traditions, the belief in the moral and spiritual values which make up part of our national heritage." Upon further questioning by Black, Daiker agreed that the prayer had a "religious facet" to it. But he noted that he did not want the Court to interpret that as meaning the board had wanted to teach religion in the schools.

"Whenever people gather together in a group and utter a prayer, a recognition of the Almighty, as has been consistently done since the founding of the country hundreds of years ago, we don't find constitutional objections," Daiker responded. "How, then," he asked, "can we say that prayer is all right on any public occasion in a State-paid-for building, with state employees, except in the school?"

Before Daiker could sit down and allow Chandler to speak, Justice Frankfurter questioned him on one final point: whether children could make up their own minds about religion. The justice related the case involving Girard College, whose founder, Stephen Girard, decreed that no one be allowed to advocate for religions on campus. Girard, a devout Catholic himself, believed that children could not critically evaluate religion until they were older and therefore should not be subjected to religious influence. The rule was challenged in court, but it was ultimately upheld.

Daiker argued that six-year-olds recited "under God" while saying the pledge to the flag, a phrase that children were well able to recognize and understand. "If Mr. Girard's argument were to prevail, he told the Court, "we would have to literally rewrite history." With that, he turned the argument over to Porter Chandler.

Chandler's Arguments

Almost immediately, Chandler drew laughter when he noted that his clients had added four more children to the case while waiting for it to be resolved. He now represented sixteen parents and their forty-one children.

His clients chose to participate in the case, Chandler said, "because they feel very strongly that it is a deprivation of their children's right to share in our national heritage." He charged the petitioners with trying "to eliminate all reference to God from the whole fabric of our public life and of our public educational system."

He disputed Butler's claim that the prayer was an attempt by the state to force religious practices onto public schoolchildren. "It is nothing of the sort," he told the Court. Rather, Chandler contended, Engel and the other parents opposed to the prayer sought to impose their views on everyone else. He accused them of trying "to drive out of the public education system practices which are long-established, venerated, and practiced without objection throughout the country from the very beginning." Students had recited prayers in New York schools since 1837, he noted.

He challenged the view that the prayer had ever been compulsory. He acknowledged that the Herricks school board had passed a resolution and "gave direction" to the principals to have students recite the prayer after the salute to the flag. But he noted, as Daiker had, that from the beginning teachers were instructed to allow students who did not want to participate to leave the room or remain silent during the prayer. After the lower court ruled that the prayer could not be compulsory, the school board adopted a formal resolution stating that fact. Even before the court ruling, Chandler noted, no student had ever been coerced into saying the prayer.

On another front, Chandler argued that the pledge, with

its "under God" phrase, was indeed a religious exercise. To make his point, he quoted a passage the House Committee issued when the phrase was added to the pledge in 1954:

Our American Government is founded on the concept of individuality and the dignity of the human being. Underlying this concept is the belief that the human person is important because he was created by God and endowed by him with certain inalienable rights which no civil authority may usurp. The inclusion of God in our pledge would further acknowledge the dependence of our people and our government upon the moral directions of the Creator.

Even with its mention of God, the pledge had been a part of students' morning ritual in every classroom in America for years, Chandler pointed out. References to God, he said, "run through our national history and our national heritage."

The Court, however, took issue with Chandler's claim that the five parents opposed all references to God or religion. A poem with the word "God" in it or the Declaration of Independence with its mention of the Creator would be acceptable because they were not practicing religion. The prayer, on the other hand, was "pinpointed at religious training."

After a few more exchanges, the red light went on and Chandler ended his argument. The justices retired to their chambers to consider the case behind closed doors while the nation waited.

OTHER RULINGS

On the same day the Supreme Court heard the *Engel* arguments, Maryland's Court of Appeals ruled that a Baltimore school had not violated the Constitution with its

Bible reading policy. As in the *Schempp* case, Bible verses were read to students every morning—followed by a recitation of the Lord's Prayer. Madalyn Murray asked school officials to excuse her son, William, from the activity. Both mother and son were atheists. The school agreed, but William became an outcast when he did not participate in the reading with the other students. Concerned, Murray sued to stop the school's Bible-reading ritual.

The policy, Murray argued, violated the First Amendment. In addition, she said, her son, who did not share the religious views expressed in the Bible, had been denied the equal protection of law guaranteed by the Fourteenth Amendment. In a four to three decision, the court denied Murray's request.

Judge William Horney, writing for the majority, explained the decision:

> Neither the First nor the Fourteenth Amendment was intended to stifle all rapport between religion and Government. The Supreme Court of the United States has not yet passed on either of the constitutional questions posed by this appeal. Yet there are several decisions concerning the separation of church and state which we think point the way and clearly indicate that a public school opening exercise such as this one— where the time and money spent on it is inconsequential—does not violate the [two amendments] as would the teaching of a sectarian religion in a public school on school time and at public expense.

Chief Judge Frederick Brune wrote the dissent for the minority. He called the Bible reading "directly contrary to the prohibition against any 'law respecting an establishment of religion,' contained in the First Amendment, as that provision has been interpreted by the Supreme Court."

This case, too, would eventually make its way to the U.S. Supreme Court.

SIX

A LANDMARK DESICION

ALMOST THREE MONTHS LATER, on June 25, 1962, the Supreme Court announced its decision in the *Engel* case. The justices, in a six to one vote, ruled the Regents' Prayer unconstitutional. Justice Hugo Black, who wrote the majority opinion, solemnly read the ruling to a waiting press corps. The reading coincided with a special ceremony marking Black's service for twenty-five terms on the Supreme Court bench.

In his ruling, Black noted that there was no doubt that the recitation of the prayer was a religious activity. By encouraging students to say the prayer, Black continued, New York state officials "adopted a practice wholly inconsistent with the Establishment Clause." The Court agreed with the parents that the prayer "breaches the constitutional wall of separation between Church and State." At the very least, Black argued, the First Amendment's ban on a state religion prohibited such prayers:

> In this country it is no part of the business of government to compose official prayers for any group of the American people to recite as a part of a religious program carried on by government.

The founders of the nation believed that government-backed religion interfered with the freedom of those who were not members of the state church even when the state did not overtly force citizens to become part of that religion. "When the power, prestige and financial support of government is placed behind a particular religious belief," Black wrote, "the indirect coercive pressure upon religious minorities to conform to the prevailing officially approved religion is plain."

But even beyond that, Black said, the founders believed the establishment clause preserved both government and religion. It was necessary to separate church and state, they believed, because "a union of government and religion tends to destroy government and to degrade religion."

In addition, Black said, the founders knew that control of religion by the state inevitably led to abuses. The justice recounted the early colonists' resistance to the edicts of the Church of England. "Governmentally established religions and religious persecutions go hand in hand," he noted. He concluded with the warning James Madison had issued when opposing Patrick Henry's proposal to establish the United States as a Christian nation: If one group could establish Christianity as the state religion, another group could as easily set up a particular sect of Christianity and exclude all other sects.

After reading the opinion, Black reminded those in the room that all Americans were free to pray in whatever way they chose. "The prayer of each man from his soul must be his and his alone. That is the genius of the First Amendment," he said. "If there is any one thing clear in the First Amendment, it is that the right of the people to pray in their own way is not to be controlled by the election returns."

A VIOLATION OF RELIGIOUS FREEDOM

In a separate, concurring decision, Justice William O. Douglas wrote that state and federal government were "honeycombed" with examples of state funding for religious exercises. He noted that the Court and the Congress started their proceedings in much the same way as New York's public schools—by invoking God's blessings. In each case, those present formed a "captive" audience. In Douglas's view, these examples and the Regents' Prayer all violated the First Amendment's ban on state-established religion.

Justice Black, in a footnote, had argued just the opposite: that the First Amendment banned only religious exercises such as the prayer, not patriotic presentations that were part of America's heritage:

> There is of course nothing in the decision reached here that is inconsistent with the fact that school children and others are officially encouraged to express love for our country by reciting historical documents such as the Declaration of Independence which contain references to the Deity or by singing officially espoused anthems which include the composer's professions of faith in a Supreme Being, or with the fact that there are many manifestations in our public life of belief in God. Such patriotic or ceremonial occasions bear no true resemblance to the unquestioned religious exercise that the State of New York has sponsored in this instance.

Douglas acknowledged that authorization of the prayer was not establishment of religion "in the strictly historical meaning of those words." Nevertheless, he concluded, by allowing such a religious exercise in the schools, government "inserts a divisive influence into our communities."

In supporting Engel, Douglas reversed his views on the previous *Everson* case, in which he voted with the majority to allow public funds for transportation to religious schools. "The *Everson* case," he wrote, "seems in retrospect to be out of line with the First Amendment." He quoted Justice Wiley B. Rutledge's dissent in the *Everson* case decrying any financial connection between state and church. "The great condition of religious liberty is that it be maintained free from sustenance, as also from other interferences, by the state," Rutledge had written.

By allowing the prayer to be recited in tax-supported schools, led by tax-paid teachers—even though the cost was minimal, the school board violated the tradition of religious freedom, Douglas concluded.

one dissent

Justice Potter Stewart issued the lone dissent. He criticized the majority opinion for using Jefferson's term "wall of separation," a phrase which, he noted, was not in the Constitution. He disagreed strongly with the majority's view that by allowing the prayer, the school board established an "official religion."

"On the contrary," Stewart argued, "I think that to deny the wish of these schoolchildren to join in reciting this prayer is to deny them the opportunity of sharing in the spiritual heritage of our Nation."

Like Douglas, Stewart listed a number of instances where God's name was invoked as part of traditional, governmental exercises. Presidents' oaths of office, Congress's opening prayers, the Court's traditional proclamation, the national anthem, and the Pledge of

Allegiance—all were part of American heritage and all contained religious references, Stewart noted.

Neither these examples nor the Regents' Prayer violated the Constitution by establishing a state religion, he concluded. Instead, they merely recognized and followed "the deeply entrenched and highly cherished spiritual traditions of our Nation—traditions which come down to us from those who almost two hundred years ago avowed their 'firm Reliance on the Protection of divine Providence' when they proclaimed the freedom and independence of this brave new world."

INTense ReacTIon

The reaction to the ruling was intense and immediate. Newspapers all over the country highlighted the news. *The New York Times* led its front-page story with the banner headline, "Supreme Court Outlaws Official School Prayers in Regents Case Decision." Other newspapers omitted the mention of "official" prayers, creating the impression that even private prayers would be banned. "School Prayer Held Illegal," read the *New York Daily News* headline. The paper's lead editorial criticized the decision. Billboards urged the impeachment of Chief Justice Earl Warren.

Southern politicians, many of whom still resented the 1954 Supreme Court ruling ordering integration in the schools, blasted

Two signs along U.S. Highway in California express opposi views of Chief Justice Earl Warr in 1963, nearly a year after t Court's *Engel* decision. The chi justice inspired deep passions Americans who either violent disagreed or adamantly support the Court's landmark decisio on religion in the schools, scho desegregation, and other issues the decision. "They put the Negroes in the schools and now they've driven God out," Representative George Andrews, D-Alabama, said. Governor Herman Talmadge of Georgia charged that the Court had "dealt a blow to all believers in a Supreme Being." Echoing the same sentiment, Senator James Eastland, D-Mississippi, called the decision a victory for "atheistic communism" that would lead to "the destruction of the religious and spiritual life of this country." North Carolina Senator Sam Ervin commented to a *New York Times* reporter, "I should like to ask whether we would be far wrong in saying that in this decision the Supreme Court has held that God is unconstitutional and for that reason the public school must be segregated against Him?" Other congressmen joined in, introducing more than one hundred bills to allow prayer in the schools.

Religious leaders, too, expressed outrage at the decision. Ironically, Catholic officials, who had once protested prayers in schools, now led the charge. "I am shocked and frightened that the Supreme Court has declared unconstitutional a simple and voluntary declaration of belief in God by public schoolchildren," said the Roman Catholic archbishop of New York, Cardinal Francis Spellman. "The decision strikes at the very heart of the Godly tradition in which America's children have for so long been raised."

Although disappointed with the ruling, school board members accepted the Supreme Court's decision as law. "The high court has now ruled and this is the purpose of our system of jurisprudence—to determine these questions," said William Vitale, president of the school board that had approved the prayer. He noted, however, that the board had never intended to infringe on students' rights. "We felt, of course, that [the prayer] would be helpful to everybody."

some support

Not all public officials opposed the ruling. Senator Philip A. Hart, D-Michigan, told CBS-Television News that he did not want his children "in a public school classroom to be exposed to someone else's religion or formula: so that I think the Supreme Court decision was right and proper." President John F. Kennedy urged calm and reminded Americans they still could pray silently. "It is important for us if we're going to maintain our constitutional principle, that we support the Supreme Court decisions, even when we may not agree with them," the president said. "In addition, we have in this case a very easy remedy, and that is to pray ourselves."

The parents who had brought the case to court rejoiced at the decision. Steven Engel and Daniel Lichtenstein told a *New York Times* reporter they were "extremely happy" with the outcome. William Butler, who had argued their cause, said the Constitution's protection of religion had allowed many different faiths to flourish in America.

parents harassed

With national attention focused on them, the parents became targets. They had to endure obscene telephone calls, threatening letters, and escalating anger. Monroe Lerner, one of the parents in the case, said neighbors refused to talk to his family because of the ruling. "We had to take our phone off the hook . . . terrible things were said to us. We got letters, with the words cut out of papers."

Steven Engel received a call at work from someone who said he had taken his children captive. "I took a taxi home from work in New York. I went to the school, but everything was OK," he reported.

Terrorists burned a large cross made of gasoline-soaked rags in the driveway of Engel's neighbor and fellow plaintiff, Lawrence Roth. People picketed with signs that said "Roth—

Godless Atheist." Callers warned that the family's car had a bomb in it and that a group called the Brooklyn Protective Association had voted to kill Roth. All five parents received a postcard that said, "You damn Jews with your liberal viewpoint are ruining a wonderful country."

Some letters, like one from a teacher, praised the families for their courage in pursuing the case. The teacher wrote: "Congratulations for the victory you have won for the United States and mankind. Your courage and determination serve as a most welcome inspiration and example to those of us who, although seeing the right, may often hesitate to capture and preserve it."

Other like-minded people helped build the Nassau Chapter of the American Civil Liberties Union, as a direct result of the case.

Years later, Engel recalled that he had hoped the matter would be settled by the school board. He said he wasn't sure he would pursue the case again, knowing the abuse his family had to endure. But, he added, "Somebody had to do it. If religious freedom was going to have any meaning in America, somebody had to do it."

MEMBERS OF THE SCHEMPP FAMILY READ FROM THE STACKS OF MAIL THEY RECEIVED AFTER FILING SUIT TO STOP RECITATION OF THE LORD'S PRAYER AND BIBLE READINGS IN PUBLIC SCHOOLS IN PHILADELPHIA. THE U.S. SUPREME COURT RULED IN 1963 THAT THE PENNSYLVANIA PRAYER READINGS VIOLATED THE FIRST AMENDMENT. FROM LEFT: SIDNEY; THE SCHEMPPS' CHILDREN, DONNA, SEVENTEEN, AND ROGER, TWENTY; AND EDWARD SCHEMPP.

SPOTLIGHT SHIFTS

The threats and protests against the families involved in the *Engel* appeal gradually died down as the spotlight shifted to other religion cases. The following term the Supreme Court heard the two cases from Pennsylvania (*Abington School District* v. *Schempp*) and

MADALYN E. MURRAY SORTS THROUGH MAIL SHE RECEIVED IN CONNECTION WITH HER SUIT TO STOP BIBLE READINGS IN THE PUBLIC SCHOOLS OF BALTIMORE. THE U.S. SUPREME COURT UPHELD HER CONTENTION THAT THE RELIGIOUS READINGS WERE UNCONSTITUTIONAL IN A RULING ISSUED IN 1963.

Maryland (*Murray* v. *Curlett*). Because they dealt with similar issues, the two cases were heard together. On June 17, 1963, the Court, in a decisive eight to one vote, struck down Pennsylvania's and Maryland's recitation of the Lord's Prayer and Bible readings. In its decision, the Court included all religious exercises under the First Amendment ban. This applied not only to those like the Regents' Prayer that had been created by officials but also to religious texts and traditional prayers.

During oral arguments, the states insisted that the practices had a secular purpose: to promote moral values, to oppose "the materialistic trends of our times," to perpetuate American institutions, and to teach literature. The Court, however, took a different view. While the First Amendment allowed Bible readings as part of a literature class, it did not permit officials to promote them as religious exercises. The decision, written by Justice Tom C. Clark, made it clear that the states had used the Bible and the Lord's Prayer for religious, not educational, purposes.

> Nothing we have said here indicates that such study of the Bible or of religion, when presented objectively as part of a secular program of education, may not be effected consistently with

the First Amendment. But the exercises here do not fall into those categories. They are religious exercises, required by the States in violation of the command of the First Amendment that the Government maintain strict neutrality, neither aiding nor opposing religion.

Clark noted the danger in allowing even "relatively minor encroachments" on religious liberty: "The breach

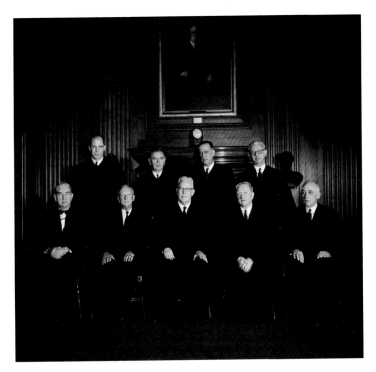

THE JUSTICES OF THE U.S. SUPREME COURT POSE FOR AN OFFICIAL PHOTOGRAPH IN JULY 1962. SEATED, FROM LEFT: JUSTICES TOM C. CLARK, HUGO L. BLACK, CHIEF JUSTICE EARL WARREN, WILLIAM O. DOUGLAS, AND JOHN M. HARLAN. STANDING, FROM LEFT: JUSTICES BYRON R. WHITE, WILLIAM J. BRENNAN JR., POTTER STEWART, AND ARTHUR J. GOLDBERG. WHITE AND GOLDBERG JOINED THE COURT AFTER THE *ENGEL* CASE HAD BEEN HEARD AND DID NOT PARTICIPATE IN THE DECISION.

of neutrality that is today a trickling stream may all too soon become a raging torrent and, in the words of Madison, 'it is proper to take alarm at the first experiment on our liberties.'"

In his opinion, Clark also dealt with the argument that banning such religious exercises interfered with the majority's free exercise of their religion, also guaranteed under the First Amendment. Even if all but one parent believed in a Bible reading, the majority could not ignore that person's rights, Clark said.

He wrote:

> While the Free Exercise Clause clearly prohibits the use of state action to deny the rights of free exercise to anyone, it has never meant that a majority could use the machinery of the State to practice its beliefs.

FUror REIGnITED

The ruling reignited the furor over religion and the schools. Churches split over the decision. Billy Graham, a world-famous American Southern Baptist minister and friend of U.S. presidents, voiced "shock" over the decision, according to a *New York Times* report the next day. Three U.S. Catholic cardinals, including New York's Francis Spellman, decried the ruling and said it would "do great harm" to the nation. Taking an opposite view, Jesuits, an ancient Catholic order, urged followers to resist any changes to the First Amendment. Several Jewish organizations and a majority of Protestant churches supported the decision.

The New York Times lauded the Court action. "It is to protect freedom of worship that the Supreme Court once

EVANGELIST BILLY GRAHAM SAID HE WAS "SHOCKED" BY THE COURT'S
DECISION IN THE *ENGEL* CASE. HE WAS AMONG THOSE WHO CONDEMNED THE
RULING. OTHER RELIGIOUS LEADERS, HOWEVER, PRAISED THE DECISION TO
KEEP GOVERNMENT OUT OF RELIGION.

again has ruled against official school prayers," the *Times* wrote in an editorial. Papers elsewhere, especially in the South, once again blasted the ban on school prayer and Bible readings.

The decision affected 41 percent of the nation's school districts in twenty-six states, where Bible readings and prayers were a regular part of morning exercises. Officials in many of those schools continued the readings in defiance of the Supreme Court order. In August the Alabama State Board of Education ordered schools in that state to read the Bible daily. That same month, officials in Arkansas followed suit. Schools in Florida and New Jersey continued Bible reading and the recitation of the Lord's Prayer until courts ordered the practices be stopped.

cases flood courts

Instead of settling the questions over the establishment clause, the *Engel* and *Schempp* cases opened the floodgates to hundreds of cases dealing with religion and the schools. For the next thirty years, supporters of school prayer sought to reverse the *Engel* decision. A few Court decisions allowed a link between government and religion, but for the most part, the Court clung to the separation policy adopted in *Engel*. Many decisions, however, showed a closely divided Court, with one vote determining the outcome.

In 1968, in *Board of Education* v. *Allen*, the Court allowed a New York law to stand. The law required local school boards to provide textbooks for all students, including those attending parochial schools. But the Court drew the line at state aid for religious schools in another case, *Lemon* v. *Kurtzman*. The case involved payments

For many, religion plays a major role in life. It helps define the reason for living, shapes a person's beliefs, and forms the basis for ethics and morals. Religion is personal; it evokes deeply felt emotions. People turn to religion for comfort when things are in turmoil. In the best scenario, religion teaches people to treat others with compassion and equality. In the worst scenario, religious leaders encourage believers to follow them blindly into battle against those with whom they disagree.

Religion has long been a weapon in the arsenal of politicians seeking to gain power. Since the dawn of religion, differences between faiths have been used to divide people and cultures. From the Christian Crusades against Muslims in the Middle Ages to the holy war proclaimed by Islamic members of al-Qaeda against Christian nations, those in power have used religion to incite followers to do their bidding.

If people think their religious beliefs are being attacked, they can and often do react emotionally. Unscrupulous leaders have used that emotion to stir up hatred and ill will toward their opponents. Even members of religions that espouse peace and harmony can react with violence, especially if their leaders encourage that behavior. They justify their actions as "doing God's work," waging a "holy war" against sin, or in other religious terms. This is particularly ironic since most religions have at their base strong bans on inflicting injury on others.

The use of religion to win political battles is one reason America's founders pushed for the separation of church and state. For more than two centuries, the First Amendment has guaranteed that each person has the right o determine how he or she will worship and that the government cannot dictate religious choices to citizens.

Despite this guarantee, however, factions have continued to use religious arguments to try to gain support for their views. Certainly that has been the case in the controversy over prayer in the schools. The issue has evoked a number of violent attacks in the name of religion. One such case in the 1980s involved the Bell family of Little Axe, Oklahoma, whose house was firebombed after they objected to the use of the public schools for prayer meetings. They ultimately won their court case against the practice, but they paid a high price for the victory. Joanne Bell, a devout member of the Nazarene church, said she received her own obituary in the mail and her children were threatened constantly.

"Religion is a highly emotional issue," said the Reverend W. W. Finlator, a Baptist pastor, at a presentation sponsored by the American Civil Liberties Union. "And the events in Little Axe are a vivid example of what happens when emotions get out of hand."

Those who use religion to promote political positions employ subtler methods to get their message across. In the 2004 election, for example, the Republican National Committee sponsored several Web sites directed at members of certain religions. The sites encouraged people of those religions to vote for Republican candidates.

Many religious leaders decry what they see as an abuse of religion by politicians. "No political party can claim that it holds the monopoly on religious morality, much less that it has received divine endorsement," said the Rev. Dr. C. Welton Gaddy, president of the non-partisan Interfaith Alliance.

The divisiveness caused by such tactics, these leaders believe, harms the nation. The answer, they say, lies not in eliminating religion or in promoting religion, but in preserving the separation between church and state. "The Establishment Clause guarantees that the government will not take sides," said the Rev. Dr. Gaddy, "and that each of us will be free to practice and teach our religion according to our individual consciences."

Only then can Americans embrace their guaranteed right to freedom of religion—and not fear that the public schools or the government will coerce their children away from their own faith.

made by Pennsylvania and Rhode Island to help fund teachers' salaries in parochial schools. Taxpayers objected to the practice and sued. The Court's 1971 ruling in the case set the standard for determining whether laws involving religion met constitutional requirements. The *Lemon* test had three parts:

- A law must have a secular (nonreligious) purpose;
- Its primary effect must neither help nor hinder religion;
- The law must not foster "an excessive government entanglement with religion."

Using the *Lemon* case as a guide, the Court allowed public school teachers to provide remedial education to disadvantaged and disabled parochial school students, as long as the lessons were not religious in any way. The Court relied on the test again when it ruled against a Louisiana law that required teachers to present the theory of "creation science" (the religious view disputing human evolution from apelike beings) when discussing evolution. The case, *Epperson* v. *Arkansas*, was decided in 1968.

In a 1980 case, *Stone* v. *Graham*, the Court ruled against the posting of the Ten Commandments in classrooms. Kentucky had required the posting but had added the notation: "The secular application of the Ten Commandments is clearly seen in its adoption as the fundamental legal code of Western Civilization and the Common Law of the United States." Even with that disclaimer, however, the Court ruled that the display was "plainly religious in nature" and did not meet the *Lemon* test.

MOMENTS OF SILENCE

After the *Engel* decision, proponents of school prayer tried other ways to include the practice in schools' morning exercises. Several states required teachers to lead students in a "moment of silence." William Butler, who had successfully argued *Engel*, noted that the requirement was just another attempt to get prayers back in the schools. He said:

> I had a law professor once who would ask, "If you call a cow's tail a leg, how many legs does it have?" And someone would always answer, "Five." But, of course, it's four, because a tail is not a leg, no matter what you call it. That's what's going on here. It's still a prayer.

The U.S. Supreme Court agreed with Butler's view. In 1985 the Court decided, in *Wallace* v. *Jaffree*, that moments of silence "for meditation or voluntary prayer" had no place in schools. The purpose behind laws requiring such practices, the Court ruled in a six to three decision, was to express "the State's endorsement of prayer activities for one minute at the beginning of each schoolday." Such endorsement, the Court decreed, "is not consistent with the established principle that the government must pursue a course of complete neutrality toward religion."

Although Justice Sandra Day O'Connor voted with the majority, she argued in her separate, concurring opinion for a much narrower restriction on moments of silence. Such practices might be allowed in public schools, she said, as long as officials did not order them as a way to promote prayer or religion. "A moment of silence is not inherently religious," O'Connor noted. And, she added, students participating in the exercise are not compelled to pray or listen to the prayers of others. Justice Lewis Powell also delivered a separate concurring opinion.

In *Wallace* and a 1984 case, *Lynch* v. *Donnelly*, O'Connor proposed modifications to the *Lemon* test. Instead of the first two parts of the *Lemon* test, O'Connor substituted her endorsement test. O'Connor's standard was not whether an event had a secular purpose but whether a "reasonable observer" would believe that the government was using the event either to endorse or disapprove of religion. In her concurrence in *Wallace*, she refined the test further:

> The endorsement test does not preclude government from acknowledging religion or from taking religion into account in making law and policy. It does preclude government from conveying or attempting to convey a message that religion or a particular religious belief is favored or preferred.

The three conservative justices on the Court favored more government support for religion than allowed under the *Lemon* test or O'Connor's endorsement clause. In a strongly worded dissent in *Wallace* v. *Jaffree*, Chief Justice William Rehnquist argued that the *Lemon* test should be abandoned altogether. Court decisions using the test, he noted, had allowed diagnostic testing at parochial schools but not treatment, transportation to the schools but not to field trips, and textbooks for students but not films for history classes. In addition, the Chief Justice said, the justices had been unable to agree on exactly how to apply the test. He pointed to the many split decisions and the number of separate opinions written by the justices.

In Rehnquist's view, the establishment clause was never meant to ensure Jefferson's "wall of separation between church and state." He dismissed the phrase that had served as a foundation for so many of the Court's religion decisions:

> The "wall of separation between church and State" is a metaphor based on bad history, a metaphor which has proved useless as a guide to judging. It should be frankly and explicitly abandoned.

Justice Anthony Kennedy proposed another test of the establishment clause in 1989. The coercion test, outlined in his dissent in *Allegheny* v. *ACLU*, allowed much more latitude for government support of religion. In his test, government could recognize and accommodate religion as long as it did not:

- Coerce anyone to "support or participate" in any religion.
- Provide "direct benefits" to a religion so as to establish a state church.

DIVISIVE ISSUE

Religion and schools continued to divide the Court. In 1992 the justices heard an appeal involving prayers by clergy at Rhode Island public school events such as graduations. School-prayer advocates hoped the case

PLEDGe: PATRIOTIC EXERCISE OR PRAYER?

The lawyers arguing for the school board in the *Engel* case used the Pledge of Allegiance as a prime example of an acceptable use of a religious term in public schools. Schoolchildren, they noted, had recited "under God" as part of the pledge for the past eight years. In arguing for *Engel*, attorney William Butler distinguished between the Regents' Prayer and the pledge. The pledge, he contended, was a political statement, not a religious exercise. Its purpose, Butler noted, was not to teach religion, but to instill patriotism.

In his concurring opinion in the case, Justice William O. Douglas put the prayer and the pledge in the same category. Both, he said, were a form of governmental aid of religion—an "unconstitutional undertaking whatever form it takes."

Francis Bellamy, an ordained minister and author, wrote the pledge in 1892. He made no mention of God in his version. Congress voted to insert the words "under God" in 1954. Senator Homer Ferguson, R-Michigan, the bill's Senate sponsor, testified that he believed the pledge "should recognize the Creator who we really believe is in control of the destinies of this great Republic." Ferguson insisted that adding God to the pledge would not violate the Constitution's ban against government establishment of religion. "This is not an attempt to establish a religion; it has nothing to do with anything of that kind," he said during hearings on the bill. Instead, according to the House report on the bill, the additional words were meant to recognize "only the guidance of God in our national affairs."

President Dwight D. Eisenhower signed the bill on Flag

Day 1954. At the time, sentiment ran high against the threat of "godless Communists." Many Americans saw the addition of God to the pledge as a symbol of America's anticommunist stance. Others, however, objected to what they viewed as an unconstitutional violation of the First Amendment's ban on government's establishment of religion. Several took their objections to court, claiming that the additional words violated the Constitution. None reached the U.S. Supreme Court until Michael Newdow's suit against Elk Grove Unified School District in 2004.

In an earlier case, the Seventh Circuit ruled that the pledge was not an example of government establishment of religion. Judge Frank Easterbrook, the author of the three-judge panel's opinion, used the same reasoning that Butler had used in the *Engel* case: "The Pledge," he wrote, "is a secular rather than sectarian vow." The 1992 decision, in *Sherman* v. *Community Consolidated School District 21*, allowed elementary students in Illinois to recite the pledge in full.

Newdow, an atheist, decided to pursue the issue. He objected to the recitation of the pledge at his daughter's school in Elk Grove, California. State law required that public school teachers lead students in reciting the Pledge of Allegiance at the beginning of each day. Students were not required to say the pledge.

Newdow claimed that the school's policy harmed his ten-year-old daughter because she was forced to "watch and listen as her state-employed teacher in her state-run school leads her classmates in a ritual proclaiming that there is a God" and that the United States is "one nation under God."

According to Newdow, the pledge as amended by Congress violated the First Amendment's establishment clause. Rather than remaining neutral in matters of religion, the government—in its pledge—touted belief in one God, he claimed. Newdow asked the U.S. District Court for the Eastern District of California to order Congress to remove the phrase "under God" from the pledge. On the opposing side, the federal government, the U.S. Congress, the president, and the school district argued that the pledge did not violate the Constitution. The district court agreed with the government and dismissed Newdow's suit.

Newdow appealed to the Ninth Circuit. On June 26, 2002, a divided court agreed with Newdow that the pledge violated the First Amendment's ban on state-sponsored religion. In a two to one decision, the three-judge panel not only ordered schools to discontinue reciting the pledge, but ruled the pledge itself unconstitutional. The ruling would have banned 9.6 million schoolchildren from saying the pledge in nine western states.

Reciting the pledge, Judge Alfred T. Goodwin stated in the majority opinion, is "to swear allegiance to the values for which the flag stands: unity, indivisibility, liberty, justice, and—since 1954—monotheism." He added:

> A profession that we are a nation "under God" is identical, for Establishment Clause purposes, to a profession that we are a nation "under Jesus," a nation "under Vishnu," a nation "under Zeus," or a nation "under no god," because none of these professions can be neutral with respect to religion.

Even though students were not required to say the pledge, Goodwin noted, the school district's policy "places students in the untenable position of choosing between participating in an exercise with religious content or protesting." Peer pressure can coerce young students to participate in classroom rituals, even if the rituals are

A firestorm of protests erupted as soon as the court announced its decision. Members of Congress stood on the steps of the Capitol and recited the pledge, shouting "under God" when they came to the phrase. They followed with a spirited rendition of "God Bless America." The decision was immediately stayed until it could be appealed. The full court later backed the panel's decision but nine judges publicly disagreed with the ruling.

In 2004, the Supreme Court agreed to hear arguments in the case. In its *amicus* brief, the state of Idaho contended that the pledge was a "patriotic exercise" and therefore did not fall under the First Amendment ban on state-sponsored religion. The brief quoted Justice William Brennan's opinion in the *Schempp* case, in which he separated the pledge from prayer:

> This general principle might also serve to insulate the various patriotic exercises and activities used in the public schools and elsewhere, which, whatever may have been their origins, no longer have a religious purpose or meaning. The reference to divinity in the revised pledge of allegiance, for example, may merely recognize the historical fact that our nation was believed to have been founded "under God."

In oral arguments, the state's lawyer pointed out that fourteen justices had referred to the pledge as a ceremonial not a religious, statement. Because the pledge had been repeated so often through the years, the lawyer noted, a "reasonable observer" would understand that it was not an invocation to a religious being. The establishment clause, he continued, did not prevent Americans from acknowledging the nation's religious heritage.

Newdow, who as a lawyer argued the case himself, said the phrase "under God" conflicted with his religious views s an atheist. "Every day my daughter is asked to stand up place her hand over her heart, and say her father is wrong," he told the justices.

Exactly fifty years after "under God" became part of the pledge, the Supreme Court, on Flag Day 2004, lifted the circuit court's ban on the pledge. The Court failed to rule, however, on whether the pledge violated the Constitution with its "under God" phrase. Instead, the Court held that Newdow did not have standing to challenge the pledge's wording. Newdow did not have primary custody of his daughter, who was the focus of the suit. Because of that, the Court did not allow Newdow to pursue his case on her behalf.

Three justices, Sandra Day O'Connor, Chief Justice William H. Rehnquist, and Clarence Thomas, wrote in concurring opinions that the pledge did not violate the establishment clause of the First Amendment. Justice Antonin Scalia did not participate in the case. He had earlier publicly criticized the Ninth Circuit's ruling on the pledge.

Observers noted that the constitutional issue will probably be addressed by the Court in the future. The Rev. Barry W. Lynn, executive director of Americans United for Separation of Church and State, said the ruling was disappointing. "The justices ducked this constitutional issue today, but it is likely to come back in the future," Lynn said. "Students should not feel compelled by school officials to subscribe to a particular religious belief in order to show love of country."

Others celebrated the decision. Elk Grove superintendent Dave Gordon termed the pledge a "unifying patriotic exercise." He said he, too, was disappointed the Court did not rule directly on the pledge. But he added, "We're grateful that our students and students throughout the country will continue to be able to recite the Pledge of Allegiance with the words 'under God,' as has been the law would lead the Court to overturn the *Lemon* decision. The Court, however, reaffirmed the *Lemon* test—but just barely. In a five to four vote, the Court banned prayers at public school events, noting that the practice was forbidden by the establishment clause. Justice Anthony Kennedy wrote the Court's majority opinion in the *Lee* v. *Weisman* case. However, papers recently released from the late Justice Harry Blackmun's files revealed that Kennedy originally sided with pro-prayer advocates in the case. After writing a draft opinion, Kennedy changed his position, according to the Blackmun papers.

After extensive revisions, Kennedy's draft became the majority opinion of the other side. In it, he stated once again that the free exercise clause of the First Amendment could not be used to override the ban on state-sponsored religious activities:

> The principle that government may accommodate the free exercise of religion does not supersede the fundamental limitations imposed by the Establishment Clause, which guarantees, at a minimum, that a government may not coerce anyone to support or participate in religion or its exercise, or otherwise act in a way which "establishes a [state] religion or religious faith, or tends to do so."

In a concurring opinion, Justice David Souter used the opportunity to challenge the coercion test and the Chief Justice's comments in the *Wallace* case. He argued that the Court should continue to oppose government endorsement of religion, even when no one is being coerced. The government, he insisted, must remain neutral in matters of religion. Justices O'Connor and Stevens joined Souter in his opinion.

In another divided decision, the Court ruled in 2000 that prayers led by students fall under the same ban as official prayers at school. Justice Stevens delivered the majority opinion in *Santa Fe School District* v. *Doe*. The case, decided by a six to three vote, involved the school district's policy of having a student say a prayer over the loudspeaker before high school football games. Students voted to have the prayer and chose the student who would deliver it. Stevens's opinion banned the policy on three grounds:

- The student prayer was not private speech (protected by the First Amendment's free-speech clause) but a public message, given on school property as a result of school policy.
- Even though the school did not force students to pray or to attend the football games, the policy was still coercive. "The Constitution demands that schools not force on students the difficult choice between whether to attend these games or to risk facing a personally offensive religious ritual," Stevens wrote.
- Having students vote on a prayer and allowing the majority to dictate religious exercises that might conflict with the views of students in the minority violated the Constitution.

seven
POLITICS AND RELIGION: A POTENT MIX

THE COURT WAS NOT ALONE in dealing with the thorny issues raised in the religion cases. Unhappy with the rulings on school prayer, opponents took their case to Congress. People's passionate response to religion created a volatile issue for politicians. Few wanted to appear opposed to the majority's religious beliefs. Those pushing for government-sanctioned religious activities used that reluctance to their advantage. They branded anyone who opposed their views as being against God, the Bible, or other popular religious icons.

The Reverend Martin Luther King Jr., the black civil rights leader well-known for praying during protests, spoke out in favor of the Court's position in *Engel*. "Its prayer decision was sound and good, reaffirming something that is basic in our Constitution, namely separation of church and state," King told a news reporter a month after the Court announced the ruling.

But many of the politicians who resisted civil rights for blacks took the opposite stand. This gave them another way to oppose the power of the Court. It also brought support from citizens in the North as well as the South.

Senate Minority Leader Everett Dirksen, who backed constitutional amendments to void both the school prayer and the school segregation rulings, used the issue to bolster his campaign against the Court. "I'm not going to let 9 men say to 190 million people, including children, when and where they can utter their prayers," Dirksen announced. This sentiment attracted black supporters as well as white. Black Christian churches played an essential role in offering support in the struggle for racial equality. Even though black citizens did not want the white majority to overrule their freedoms, many believed the Christian majority should rule on the issue of prayer in the schools. Within months of the *Engel* decision, groups had organized opposition to the school prayer ruling across the country. One conservative Christian group, Project America, presented Congress with a petition signed by more than one million people. Politicians responded quickly to the groundswell of protests. In April 1964 Congress began hearings on 144 resolutions to amend the Constitution to allow Bible readings and prayers in public schools. Momentum for a constitutional amendment slowed, however, as churches and other groups took stands against the action. The United Presbyterian Church, the Episcopal Church, the American Jewish Congress, and the Southern and American Baptist Conventions all voted against such efforts. On April 29, 1964, representatives from more than thirty Christian denominations appeared before the House Judiciary Committee in support of the Supreme Court decisions in the matter.

Although Congress eventually dropped the proposals, new resolutions to allow prayers and Bible readings in school reappeared periodically. In 1966, the Senate failed by nine votes to pass a school prayer amendment. The House defeated a similar resolution in 1971, twenty-eight votes short of the two-thirds majority needed. Several years later Senator Jesse Helms (R-North Carolina) proposed an amendment that would bar federal courts from hearing state cases on school prayer. Congress defeated the Helms Amendment in 1980, in part because it threatened the balance of power.

During the 1980s President Ronald Reagan pushed for a constitutional amendment allowing prayers in public schools. The resolution, submitted to Congress on May 17, 1982, read: "Nothing in this Constitution shall be construed to prohibit individual or group prayer in public schools or other public institutions. No person shall be required by the United States or by any state to participate in prayer. Neither the United States nor any state shall compose the words of any prayer to be said in public schools." The Senate defeated the measure two years later, when it failed to win a two-thirds majority by eleven votes. However, during the campaign to get it passed, Reagan's vice president, George H. Bush, convinced the Southern Baptist Convention, which had always supported separation of church and state, to endorse the amendment.

In 1997 the House of Representatives passed a resolution to "promote the display of the Ten Commandments on public property." This directly opposed the Supreme Court's 1980 ruling against such a practice. The resolution, passed by a vote of 295 to 125, had no power to change laws or affect court rulings.

Free Speech v. Religious Freedom

Responding to what he called "the public's valid concern that our courts have become hostile to religion, Representative Ernest J. Istook Jr., R-Oklahoma, submitted the Religious Freedom Amendment of 1999. More than one hundred and fifty members of Congress cosponsored the bill. Istook framed the battle as one of free speech. He insisted that the Court's rulings on school prayer placed "barriers to religious expression which do not exist for other forms of free speech." The House of Representatives voted 224 to 203 to support the amendment, sixty-six votes short of the two-thirds majority required.

After the September 11, 2001, terrorist attacks on the Pentagon and the World Trade Center, school-prayer advocates seized the opportunity to present a resolution to Congress. The legislation, sponsored by Representative Walter B. Jones Jr., R-North Carolina, proposed that schools set aside time for children to pray or reflect quietly "during this time of struggle against the forces of international terrorism." The measure passed the House and was referred to the Senate for consideration. It languished in a Senate subcommittee, where no further action was taken after November 2001.

Istook reintroduced his amendment in 2003. President George W. Bush was among those urging its passage. The text of the new school prayer amendment read:

Proposing an amendment to the Constitution of the United States restoring religious freedom (House Joint Resolution 46)

Resolved by the Senate and House of Representatives of the United States of America in Congress assembled (two-thirds of each House concurring therein), That the following article is proposed as an amendment to the Constitution of the United States, which shall be valid to all intents and purposes as part of the Constitution when ratified by the legislatures of three-fourths of the several States within seven years after the date of its submission for ratification, and is intended to include protection of the Pledge of Allegiance to the Flag, the display of the Ten Commandments, and voluntary school prayer:

Article—

To secure the people's right to acknowledge God according to the dictates of conscience:

The people retain the right to pray and to recognize

their religious beliefs, heritage, and traditions on
public property, including schools.
The United States and the States shall not establish
any official religion nor require any person to join
in prayer or religious activity.

Congress also considered two similar measures calling
for a constitutional amendment to allow school prayer. All
three were referred to House subcommittees for review
before being considered for a vote. In May 2003, Istook's
proposal was referred to the House Subcommittee on the
Constitution. As of November 2004, no further action had
been taken on any of the bills.

Representative Istook said the Supreme Court rulings
on school prayer and other religious issues "have provoked
public outrage since 1962" when the *Engel* decision was
delivered. He noted that polls showed that 75 percent of
Americans favored a constitutional amendment to allow
prayer in public schools. If passed, the Istook amendment
would overturn all or parts of *Engel, Abington, Wallace,
Lee, Stone, Lemon,* and many other rulings on religion. It
would allow prayers in the classroom on a voluntary basis,
permit schools to set aside moments of silence for
reflection and prayer, and allow the majority to choose the
form and content of religious exercises at public events.

"Under the pretense of promoting tolerance, our
courts have . . . been used to promote censorship," Istook
wrote in his analysis of the proposed legislation. The
amendment, he said, would fulfill the intentions of the
Constitution— "to protect each and every one of us, not
merely some of us."

Representative Chet Edwards (D-Texas), who led
the effort to defeat the measure in 1998, called the
amendment a "horrible solution in search of a problem."
Opponents, including a coalition of religious and
civil rights groups and most Democrats, criticized the

proposal as unnecessary and dangerous. Rabbi David Saperstein, representing the Union of American Hebrew Congregations and the Central Conference of American Rabbis, wrote of his objections to the House Judiciary Committee. "The Amendment would deal a devastating blow to religious freedom and religious tolerance in America," he said.

Thirteen Democratic members of Congress issued their own statement against the Istook amendment. If the measure were adopted, they said, schoolchildren and others in public places would be forced to pray as the government required; taxpayers would have to support schools operated by religions they disagreed with; and religious freedom would become a thing of the past. The statement concluded:

> We are deeply troubled over the notion of amending the First Amendment, which has stood as a bulwark of our democratic system of government. The freedom of religion established by the First Amendment is one of the fundamentals on which our country was founded. Religious freedom separates our country from all others and has worked to protect our citizens' freedom for over 200 years. Now is not the time to alter the constitutional structure which underlies this freedom.

campaign issue

Since the Reagan era, the religious right and conservative Republicans have united behind the school prayer issue. They have used the issue of prayer (and Bible readings) in schools to win support against political opponents. Speakers for their cause have blamed the *Engel* decision for everything from drug use to rude behavior in the schools. During the 2004 presidential election, the

Republican National Committee sent mass mailings to voters in Arkansas and West Virginia warning that liberal Democrats would ban the Bible if elected.

In other political maneuvering leading up to the 2004 elections, Republicans in the House of Representatives pushed through a bill that would prevent federal courts from ruling on constitutional issues raised by bills to ban gay marriage. The same tactic had been used unsuccessfully to bar the courts from reviewing laws on school prayer, the Pledge of Allegiance to the Flag, and

U.S. CONGRESSMAN BARNEY FRANK, D-MASSACHUSETTS, ADDRESSES THE 2004 DEMOCRATIC PRESIDENTIAL CONVENTION IN BOSTON. FRANK LED THE FIGHT AGAINST A BILL THAT WOULD HAVE DENIED THE COURTS THE RIGHT TO RULE ON CONSTITUTIONAL ISSUES RAISED BY BILLS TO BAN GAY MARRIAGE.

U.S. Attorney General John Ashcroft speaks at a ceremony to dedicate the new Oklahoma City federal building in May 2004. Ashcroft, one of the most conservative members of the first George W. Bush administration, during his tenure in office urged reinstating prayers in public schools.

other controversial issues. In the past, however, neither House nor Senate has mustered enough votes to pass such a bill. The House's support of the bill this time concerned proponents of civil rights and religious freedom. *The New York Times* called the House action "a radical assault on the Constitution" that would "upset the system of checks and balances and threaten all minority groups." Opponents said attempts to deprive the courts of authority were unconstitutional, much like the Helms Amendment more than two decades earlier. Passage of the bill would "make the biggest hole in the United States Constitution that we have seen since we became one Nation," Representative Barney Frank, D-Massachusetts, told colleagues during a House debate on the bill.

It was doubtful that the bill would win enough votes in the Senate to become law. But the campaign illustrated the continuing efforts to prevent courts, including the U.S. Supreme Court, from ruling against conservative positions.

Engel STILL LAW

Despite the passionate and determined efforts of the school-prayer forces for more than forty years, Congress has not passed a constitutional amendment on the issue, and the Court has not overturned the *Engel* decision. Bertram Daiker, the attorney who argued for school prayer in the *Engel* case, believes the 1962 decision was not justified. "I thought the Court was wrong then, and I still think it was wrong," he said.

But he doesn't think *Engel* will be reversed in the near future. "We seem to be on the defensive as to where we can say God or mention our religious heritage. But I don't think there's a great upsurge to change things."

William Butler, the ACLU lawyer who won the case, agrees with that assessment. "I think it's written in stone, *Engel* v. *Vitale*," he said. "I don't think it's possible to tinker around with the First Amendment nowadays. If the First Amendment came up today, it wouldn't pass. Thank God we are stuck with it."

TImeLIne

1930
The Supreme Court allowed states to buy nonreligious textbooks for students at parochial schools in *Cochran* v. *Louisiana State Board of Education*. The expenditure, the Court reasoned, benefited society by providing educated citizens.

1940
In *Minersville School District* v. *Gobitis*, the Supreme Court ruled that national unity overruled religious freedom in deciding that school-children were required to say the Pledge of Allegiance even if it violated their religious beliefs.

1943
The Supreme Court overturned the *Gobitis* decision in *West Virginia State Board of Education* v. *Barnette*. This time the Court ruled that under the First Amendment children could not be compelled to salute the flag.

1947
Everson v. *Board of Education* tightened rules on how taxpayers' money could be spent for students at religious schools. The Court ruled that the local school board could give parents money to cover their children's transportation costs to parochial schools.

1948
In *McCollum* v. *Board of Education*, the Supreme Court ruled that an Illinois school board violated the Constitution when it allowed religion classes to be held in its schools.

1952
In *Zorach* v. *Clauson*, the Supreme Court upheld the constitutionality

of a New York law that allowed students to be excused from school to attend religious classes elsewhere.

1962
The Supreme Court ruled, in *Engel* v. *Vitale*, that a school policy of reciting a nonsectarian prayer written by the New York Board of Regents was unconstitutional.

1963
The Supreme Court, in a ruling joining two cases—*Abington Township School District* v. *Schempp* and *Murray* v. *Curlett*, banned religious exercises, including prayers and Bible readings, in public schools.

1968
The Court's ruling in *Board of Education* v. *Allen* allowed textbooks to be provided for all students, including those attending parochial schools.

1968
In *Epperson* v. *Arkansas*, the Supreme Court held unconstitutional the Arkansas law that required the teaching of creationism (the religious teaching that humans did not descend from apelike creatures) in addition to Charles Darwin's theory of evolution in public schools.

1971
Lemon v. *Kurtzman* set the standards by which to judge whether laws involving religion met Constitutional requirements.

1972
The Court decided, in *Wisconsin* v. *Yoder*, that a state could override a citizen's religious liberty only when it had a compelling interest, one that could not be achieved otherwise. In the case, the Court ruled that Amish children did not have to attend public school beyond the eighth grade.

1980
In *Stone* v. *Graham*, the Supreme Court ruled the posting of the Ten Commandments in public schools unconstitutional. The case involved a Kentucky law that required the posting in every classroom in the state.

1985
According to the Court's decision in *Wallace* v. *Jaffree*, the state did not maintain neutrality toward religion as required by the First Amendment. The Court declared unconstitutional Alabama's law providing for a moment of silence for meditation or voluntary prayer in the public schools.

1992

In *Lee* v. *Weisman* the Court ruled that the Constitution bars prayers said by clergy invited by officials to give the convocation at graduations and other public school functions.

2000

In *Sante Fe School District* v. *Doe*, the Court barred student-led prayers in public schools. The prayers, according to the decision, fell under the same restrictions as official prayers.

2004

Elk Grove United School District v. *Newdow* marked the first time the Supreme Court heard a case on the "under God" phrase inserted into the Pledge of Allegiance by Congress in 1954. The Court declined to rule on the constitutionality of reciting the pledge in public schools when it dismissed the case because Michael Newdow lacked standing.

NOTES

FOREWORD

p. 7, par. 1, Amendment 1, U.S. Constitution.

p. 8, par. 3, James Madison. "Memorial and Remonstrance, 1785."

p. 11, par. 3, Robert S. Alley. *School Prayer: The Court, the Congress, and the First Amendment*. New York: Prometheus Books, 1994.

p. 11, par. 4, *Engel v. Vitale*, 370 U.S. 421 (1962), majority opinion.

Chapter 1

p. 12, par. 2, "Regents' Prayer," *Engel v. Vitale*, 370 U.S. 421 (1962).

p. 13, par. 3, "Debate 6 — Prayer in Public Schools." Pearson/Prentice Hall http://www.graves.k12.ky.us/schools/GCHS/bleonard/HTML/d/debate6.htm

p. 13, par. 4, Fred W. Friendly and Martha J. H. Elliott. *The Constitution: That Delicate Balance*. New York: Random House, 1984, p. 110.

p. 14, par. 1, George DeWan. "School Prayer Divides LI," *Newsday*, 2004.

p. 15, par. 3–p. 16, par. 1, Friendly and Elliott. *The Constitution: That Delicate Balance*, pp. 118–119.

p. 16, par. 4, *The New York Times*, June 28, 1962, p. 17.

Chapter 2

p. 18, par. 2, *The Religious History of New England*. Cambridge, Massachusetts: Harvard University Press, 1917, p. 13.

p. 19, par. 2, Sydney E. Ahlstrom. *A Religious History of the American People*. New Haven: Yale University Press, 1972, pp. 166, 154.

p. 21, par. 2, Articles of Confederation.

p. 22, par. 3, U.S. Constitution, Article VI.

p. 22, par. 3, Arthur S. Link, Robert V. Remini, Douglas Greenberg, and Robert C. McMath Jr. *A Concise History of the American People*. Arlington Heights, IL: Harlan Davidson, 1984, p. A—8.

p. 23, par. 4–p. 24, par.1, Library of Congress. "Religion and the Founding of the American Republic" http://adam2.org/articles/lib_congress_exhibit/relo5.html

p. 24, par. 2, Susan Dunn. "The Inquisition in Alabama," *Christian Science Monitor*, August 28, 2003.

p. 24, par. 4–5, James Madison. "Memorial and Remonstrance Against Religious Assessments," 1785.

p. 25, par. 1, Dunn. "The Inquisition in Alabama."

p. 25, par. 3, Thomas Jefferson. "Bill for Establishing Religious Freedom," 1786.

p. 25, par. 4, Ann E. Weiss. *God and Government: The Separation of Church and State*. Boston: Houghton Mifflin, 1982, pp. 29, 30.

p. 25, par. 5–p. 26, par.1, First Amendment, U.S. Constitution.

p. 26, par. 3, Moses Seixas. "Letter to President George Washington," 1789.

p. 26, par. 4–p. 27, par. 3, George Washington. "Letter to Touro Synagogue," 1789.

p. 27, par. 3, George Washington. *Thanksgiving Proclamation*, 1789.

p. 28, par. 1, Junto Society. "Presidential inaugural speeches." http://www.juntosociety.com/inaugural/jadams.html.

p. 28, par. 1, James Haught. *2000 Years of Disbelief: Famous People With the Courage to Doubt*. Amherst, NY: Prometheus Books, 1996.

p. 28, par. 1, "The Barbary Treaties: Treaty of Peace and Friendship, Signed at Tripoli November 4, 1796." The Avalon Project. http://www.yale.edu/lawweb/avalon/diplomacy/barbary/bar 1796t.htm.

p. 28, par. 1, Rob Boston. *Why the Religious Right is Wrong About Separation of Church and State*. Amherst, NY: Prometheus Books, 1994, pp. 78–79.

p. 28, par. 2–p. 29, par. 1, June 12, 1812, Letter of John Adams to Benjamin Rush, quoted in *The Spur of Fame*, J. A. Schutz, and D. Adair, eds. San Marino, CA: The Huntington Library, 1966, p. 224.

p. 29, par. 2, Thomas Paine, *Age of Reason*, 1795; "Declaration of the Rights of Man," 1789.

p. 29, par. 3–4, Thomas Jefferson, Letter to Horatio Spafford, 1814.

p. 30, par. 2–3, Address of the Danbury Baptist Association in the State of Connecticut assembled October 7, 1801, to Thomas Jefferson, Esq., President of the United States of America.

p. 30, par. 4, Thomas Jefferson, Letter to the Danbury Baptist Association, January 1, 1802.

p. 32, par. 2, National Museum of American Jewish History. http://nmajh.org/

p. 32, par. 3, American Protective Association Statement of Principles, 1894, cited in "The American Protective Association," Pam Epstein. http://projects.vassar.edu/1896/apa.html.

p. 32, par. 4, Samuel F. B. Morse, *Imminent Dangers to the Free Institutions of the United States through Foreign Immigration* (1835). New York: Arno Press, Inc., 1969, pp. 6–15.

p. 33, par. 1, Stephan F. Brumberg. "The Cincinnati Bible War," *HUC Journal*, vol. LIV.2, April 29, 2004, p. 12.

p. 33, par. 1, Julie Byrne. "Roman Catholics and Immigration in Nineteenth–Century America," National Humanities Center. http://www.nhc.rtp.nc.us:8080/tserve/nineteen/nkeyinfo/nromcath.htm

pp. 34–35, "The Bible in the Schools," *The New York Times*, Nov. 29, 1871, p. 1.

p. 36, par. 1, Victoria Sherrow. *Separation of Church and State*. New York: Franklin Watts, 1992, p. 32.

p. 36, par. 2, Israelite, January 8, 1869, p. 4, cited in "The Cincinnati Bible War," Stephan F. Brumberg, *HUC Journal*, vol. LIV.2, April 29, 2004, p. 23.

p. 36, par. 2, Joan DelFattore. *The Fourth R: Conflicts Over Religion in America's Public Schools*. New Haven, CT: Yale University Press, 2004, p. 140–141

p. 36, par. 3–p.37, par. 1 *Permoli* v. *Municipality No. 1 of the City of New Orleans*, 44 U.S. 589 (1845).

p. 37, par. 3–5, Fourteenth Amendment, U.S. Constitution.

p. 37, par. 6, Jethro K. Lieberman. *Milestones! Two Hundred Years of American Law*. New York: Oxford University Press, 1976, p. 333.

Chapter 3

p. 38, par. 3, *Reynolds* v. *United States*, 98 U.S. 145 (1878).

p. 39, par. 1, *Davis* v. *Beason*, 133 US 333 (1890).

p. 39, par. 4–p. 40, par. 1, "Words and Deeds in American History," Letter, Billy Gobitas to Minersville, Pennsylvania, school directors, 1935. William Gobitas Papers, Library of Congress, http://memory.loc.gov/ammem.

p. 40, par. 3, *Minersville School District* v. *Gobitis*, Court of Appeals for the Third Circuit, 1938, Olin R. Moyle brief.

p. 40, par. 5, Ibid., majority opinion.

p. 41, par. 1–p. 42, par. 1, *Minersville School District* v. *Gobitis*, 310 U.S. 586 (1940), majority opinion.

p. 43, par. 1–4; p. 46, par. 1, Ibid., dissent.

p. 45, par. 6–p. 46, par. 1, *West Virginia State Board of Education* v. *Barnette*, 319 US 624 (1943), majority opinion.

p. 47, par. 6–p. 48, par. 1, *Wisconsin* v. *Yoder*, 406 US 205 (1972).

p. 48, par. 3–p. 49, par. 2, Stephan F. Brumberg. "The Cincinnati Bible War," *HUC Journal*, vol. LIV.2, April 29, 2004, p. 23.

p. 49, par. 4–p. 50, par. 3, *The Bible in the Public Schools. Arguments Before the Superior Court of Cincinnati in the Case of* Minor v. Board of Education of Cincinnati (1870) *with the Opinions of the Court and the Opinion on Appeal of the Supreme Court of Ohio.* New York: Da Capo Press, 1967.

p. 50, par. 4–p. 51, par. 1, *People ex rel. Ring* v. *Board of Education*, 245 Ill. 334, 351 (1910).

p. 51, par. 5, *American State Papers Bearing on Sunday Legislation*, 1st edition. Compiled and Annotated by William Addison Blakely, (1890); and 2nd edition, Willard Colcord, ed. Washington, DC: by The Religious Liberty Association, 1911, pp 341–343. Cited in "The NRA (National Reform Association) and the Christian Amendment" by Jim Allison. http://members.tripod.com/~candst/nra.htm.

p. 52–54, U.S. Government Printing Office http://www.gpoaccess.gov/constitution/browse.html; U.S. National Archives & Records Administration, Federal Register "The Constitutional Amendment Process" http://www.archives.gov/federal_register/constitution/amendment_process.html; and The U.S. Constitution Online http://www.usconstitution.net/constamprop.html.

p. 55, par. 2–3, Steven Keith Green. "The National Reform Association and the Religious Amendments to the Constitution, 1864–1876." An unpublished masters thesis, University of North Carolina at Chapel Hill, 1987, p. 50. Cited in "The NRA (National Reform Association) and the Christian Amendment." http://members.tripod.com/~candst/nra.htm.

p. 55, par. 4, "Is America A 'Christian Nation'? Religion, Government And Individual Freedom." Americans United For Separation of Church and State. http://www.au.org/site/DocServer/Is_the_United_States_a_Christian_nation.pdf?docID=103.

p. 57, par. 2, *Everson* v. *Board of Education of Ewing TP.*, 330 U.S. 1 (1947), majority opinion.

p. 57, par. 3, *Everson* v. *Board of Education of Ewing TP.*, 330 U.S. 1 (1947), Justice Robert Jackson dissent.

p. 57, par. 3–p. 58, par. 1, *Everson* v. *Board of Education of Ewing TP.*, 330 U.S. 1 (1947), Justice Wiley B. Rutledge dissent.

p. 58, par. 3, Vashti Cromwell McCollum. *One Woman's Fight.* Madison, WI: Freedom From Religion Foundation Inc., 1993.

p. 58, par. 6–p. 59, par. 3, *McCollum* v. *Board of Education*, 333 U.S. 203 (1948), majority opinion.

p. 59, par. 4; p. 64, par. 1, *McCollum* v. *Board of Education*, 333 U.S. 203 (1948), Justice Felix Frankfurter concurring opinion.

p. 64, par. 4–p. 65, par. 1, *Zorach* v. *Clauson*, 343 U.S. 306 (1952), majority opinion.

p. 65, par. 2, *Zorach* v. *Clauson*, 343 U.S. 306 (1952), Justice Hugo Black dissent.

p. 65, par. 3, *Zorach* v. *Clauson*,, 343 U.S. 306 (1952), Justice Robert Jackson dissent.

Chapter 4

p. 66, par. 2, "William J. Butler." Urban Morgan Institute for Human Rights, Cincinnati, Ohio.
http://www.law.uc.edu/morgan/butler01/butlerbio.html

p. 66, par. 3, Fred W. Friendly and Martha J. H. Elliott. *The Constitution: That Delicate Balance.* New York: Random House, 1984, p. 118.

p. 67, par. 2, Roy R. Silver. "5 L.I. Parents Who Started Suit Hail Decision," *The New York Times*, June 26, 1962, p. 17.

p. 67, par. 4–p. 68, par. 2, Friendly and Elliott. *The Constitution: That Delicate Balance*, p. 120.

p. 68, par. 3, Ibid.

p. 68, par. 5, Ibid., p. 121.

p. 69, par. 2–4, Philip B. Kurland and Gerhard Casper. *Landmark Briefs and Arguments of the Supreme Court of the United States: Constitutional Law,* "*Engel* v. *Vitale*," vol. 56. Arlington, VA: University Publications of America Inc., 1975, p. 770.

p. 69, par. 7, Ibid., p. 866.

p. 69, par. 8–p. 70, par. 2, "The Justices' Caseload." Supreme Court of the United States booklet. Washington, DC: Supreme Court Historical Society.

p. 70, par. 3, Friendly and Elliott. *The Constitution: That Delicate Balance*, p. 121.

p. 70, par. 4, Ibid., p. 119.

pp. 71–73, Iowa Court Information System.
http://www.judicial.state.ia.us/students/6 (Accessed Nov. 3, 2003); The Supreme Court Historical Society
http://www.supremecourthistory.org (Accessed Nov. 3, 2003); Administrative Office of the U.S. Courts
http://www.uscourts.gov (Accessed Nov. 3, 2003)

p. 75, par. 2–3, Kurland and Casper. *Landmark Briefs and Arguments of the Supreme Court of the United States: Constitutional Law,* "*Engel* v. *Vitale*," Butler's brief.

p. 75, par. 4–p. 76, par. 2, Ibid., Daiker's brief.

p. 76, par. 4, Ibid., Board of Regents *amicus* brief.

p. 77, par. 5–p. 78 , par. 1, William G. Weart. "Bible in Schools Curbed by Court," *The New York Times*, Feb. 2, 1962, p. 31.

Chapter 5

p. 80, par. 2–3, Author's interview with Bertram B. Daiker, September 1, 2004.

p. 80, par. 6, "The Court and Its Procedures," Supreme Court of the United States booklet. Washington, DC: Supreme Court Historical Society.

p. 83, par. 1, Tom Wicker. *Dwight D. Eisenhower.* New York: Times Books/Henry Holt & Company, 2002.

p. 84, par. 2, William E. Nelson. *Marbury* v. *Madison: The Origins and Legacy of Judicial Review.* Lawrence: University Press of Kansas, 2000.

p. 84, par. 4–p. 95, par. 4, *Engel* v. *Vitale,* 370 U.S. 421 (1962), oral arguments.

p. 96, par. 4–p. 97, par. 1, "Maryland Backs Prayer in School; Baltimore Practice Upheld by State High Court, 4 to 3 Two Amendments Cited Chief Judge Dissents New York Prayer Upheld," *The New York Times,* April 7, 1962, p. 14.

Chapter 6

p. 98, par. 2–p. 99, par. 3, *Engel* v. *Vitale,* 370 U.S. 421 (1962), majority opinion.

p. 99, par. 4, Anthony Lewis. "Supreme Court Outlaws Official School Prayers in Regents Case Decision," *The New York Times,* June 25, 1962, p. 1.

p. 100, par. 1, *Engel* v. *Vitale,* 370 U.S. 421 (1962), Justice William O. Douglas, concurring opinion.

p. 100, par. 3, *Engel* v. *Vitale,* 370 U.S. 421 (1962), majority opinion.

p. 100, par. 4–p. 101, par. 2, *Engel* v. *Vitale,* 370 U.S. 421 (1962), Justice William O. Douglas, concurring opinion.

p. 101, par. 2, *Everson* v. *Board of Education of Ewing TP.,* 330 U.S. 1 (1947), Justice Wiley B. Rutledge dissent, cited in *Engel* v. *Vitale,* 370 U.S. 421 (1962), Justice William O. Douglas, concurring opinion.

p. 101, par. 4–p. 102, par. 2, *Engel* v. *Vitale,* 370 U.S. 421 (1962), Justice Potter Stewart, dissent.

p. 103, par. 1, Anthony Lewis. "Supreme Court Outlaws Official School Prayers in Regents Case Decision."

p. 103, par. 1, Anthony Lewis. "Court Again Under Fire," *The New York Times,* July 1, 1962, p. 114.

p. 103, par. 2, George DeWan. "School Prayer Divides LI," *Newsday,* 2004.

p. 103, par. 3, Roy R. Silver. "5 L.I. Parents Who Started Suit Hail Decision," *The New York Times,* June 26, 1962, p. 17.

p. 104, par. 1, "CBS Reports: Storm Over the Supreme Court," March 13, 1963, transcript, cited in *The Constitution: That Delicate Balance.*

p. 104, par. 2, Roy R. Silver. "5 L.I. Parents Who Started Suit Hail Decision," *The New York Times,* June 26, 1962, p. 17.

p. 104, par. 3–4, George DeWan. "School Prayer Divides LI."

p. 104, par. 5–p. 105, par. 1, Fred W. Friendly and Martha J. H. Elliott. *The Constitution: That Delicate Balance*. New York: Random House, 1984, p. 126.

p. 105, par. 1–par. 4, George DeWan. "School Prayer Divides LI."

p. 105, par. 5–p. 108, par. 4, *Abington School District* v. *Schempp*, 374 U.S. 203 (1963), majority opinion.

p. 108, par. 5, Alexander Burnham. "Edict Is Called a Setback by Christian Clerics Rabbis Praise It; Churchmen Voice Shock at Ruling," *The New York Times*, June 26, 1962, p. 1.

p. 108, par. 6–p. 109, par.1, *The New York Times*, June 26, 1962.

pp. 111–113, "America's Constitutional Heritage: Religion and Our Public Schools," video, American Civil Liberties Union.
http://www.lectlaw.com/files/con23.htm

p. 114, par. 2–4, *Lemon* v. *Kurtzman*, 403 U.S. 602 (1971), majority opinion.

p. 114, par. 6, *Stone* v. *Graham*, 449 U.S. 39 (1980).

p. 115, par. 2, Friendly and Elliott. *The Constitution: That Delicate Balance*, p. 126.

p. 115, par. 3, *Wallace* v. *Jaffree*, 472 U.S. 38 (1985).

p. 115, par. 4–p. 116, par. 3, *Wallace* v. *Jaffree*, 472 U.S. 38 (1985), Justice Sandra Day O'Connor concurring opinion.

p. 116, par. 4–p. 117, par. 3, *Wallace* v. *Jaffree*, 472 U.S. 38 (1985), Chief Justice William H. Rehnquist, dissent.

p. 117, par. 5–6, *Allegheny* v. *ACLU*, 492 US 573 (1989).

pp. 118–122, David Stout. "Court Ruling Keeps Pledge Intact but Leaves 'God' Issue Unsettled," *The New York Times*, June 14, 2004. Jeffrey Owen Jones. "The Pledge's Creator." *The Smithsonian Magazine*, November 2003.
Michael A. Newdow v. *Elk Grove Unified School District et al*, United States Court of Appeals for the Ninth Circuit, No. 00–16423.
Associated Press. "High court: Atheist can't challenge 'God' in Pledge," June 14, 2004.
CNN, "Court dismisses Pledge case," June 15, 2004.
Elk Grove Unified School District and David W. Gordon v. *Michael A. Newdow et al*, No. 02–1624, U.S. Supreme Court, oral arguments, briefs, majority opinion, concurring opinions.
Evelyn Nieves, "Judges Ban Pledge of Allegiance From Schools, Citing 'Under God'," *The New York Times*, June 27, 2002, Section A, p. 1.

p. 117, par. 7; p. 123, par. 1, Nina Totenberg. "Profile: Papers of former Supreme Court Justice Harry Blackmun," National Public Radio, March 7, 2004.

p. 123, par. 4, *Lee v. Weisman*, 505 U.S. 577 (1992), majority opinion.
p. 123, par. 4, *Lee v. Weisman*, 505 U.S. 577 (1992), Justice David Souter concurring opinion.
p. 124, par. 2–4, *Santa Fe Independent School District* v. *Doe* (99–62) 530 U.S. 290 (2000).

Chapter 7
p. 125, par. 2, Jonathan Zimmerman. "The Other Massive Resistance: School Prayer and the Conservative Revolution, 1962–1984." Director, History of Education Program, New York University, January 25, 2001.
p. 125, par. 4–p. 126, par. 1, Ibid.
p. 126, par. 3, Ibid.
p. 126, par. 4–p. 127, par. 1, Lawrence J. McAndrews. "'Moral' Victories: Ronald Reagan and the Debate over School Prayer," *Religion & Education*, Spring 2003, Vol. 30, No. 1.
p. 127, par. 1, Robert S. Alley. *School Prayer: The Court, the Congress, and the First Amendment*. New York: Prometheus Books, 1994, p. 193.
p. 127, par. 3, U.S. Representative Ernest J. Istook Jr. "Detailed and Legal Analysis Of the Religious Freedom Amendment House Joint Resolution 78." Library of Congress.
p. 128, par. 1, "House Rpt. 105–543 – Proposing an Amendment to the Constitution of the United States Restoring Religious Freedom." Library of Congress.
p. 128, par. 3–p. 129, par. 1, "Proposing an amendment to the Constitution of the United States restoring religious freedom. H. J. RES. 46." Library of Congress.
p. 129, par. 3–4, U.S. Representative Ernest J. Istook Jr. "Detailed and Legal Analysis Of the Religious Freedom Amendment House Joint Resolution 78." Library of Congress.
p. 129, par. 5–p. 130, par. 1, Daniel Kurtzman. "News Analysis: School–religion amendment fails, but the fight is long from finished," *Jewish Telegraphic Agency*, June 12, 1998.
p. 129, par. 5–p. 130, par. 1, "National Organizations Oppose Istook Amendment," Relgious Action Center of Reform Judaism, March 3, 1998.
p. 130, par. 3, "House Rpt. 105–543 – Proposing an Amendment to the Constitution of the United States Restoring Religious Freedom."
p. 130, par. 2–3, Ibid.

p. 130, par. 4–p. 131, par. 1, David D. Kirkpatrick. "THE 2004 CAMPAIGN: THE TACTICS; Republicans Admit Mailing Campaign Literature Saying Liberals Will Ban the Bible," *The New York Times*, September 24, 2004, Section A , p. 22.

p. 131, par. 2–p. 133, par. 1, "A Radical Assault on the Constitution," *The New York Times*, July 24, 2004, Section A , p. 12.

p. 131, par. 2–p. 133, par. 1, "Providing for Consideration of H.R. 3313, Marriage Protection Act of 2004," House of Representatives, July 22, 2004, Congressional Record, p. H6569.

p. 133, par. 3–4, Author's interview with Bertram B. Daiker, September 1, 2004.

p. 133, par. 5, George DeWan. "School Prayer Divides LI," *Newsday*, 2004.

p. 133, par. 5, Fred W. Friendly, and Martha J. H. Elliott. *The Constitution: That Delicate Balance*. New York: Random House, 1984, p. 126.

FurTHer InformaTion

FURTHER READING

Andryszewski, Tricia. *School Prayer: A History of the Debate* (Issues in Focus). Berkeley Heights, NJ: Enslow Publishers, 1997.

Bernstein, Richard. *Thomas Jefferson and the Revolution of Ideas* (Oxford Portraits). New York: Oxford University Press, 2004.

Farber, Daniel. *The First Amendment* (Concepts & Insights). New York: Foundation Press, 2002.

Farish, Leah. *The First Amendment: Freedom of Speech, Religion, and the Press.* Berkeley Heights, NJ: Enslow Publishers, 1998.

Foner, Eric. *The Story of American Freedom.* New York: W. W. Norton & Company, 1999.

Gaustad, Edwin S. *Church and State in America* (Religion in American Life). New York: Oxford University Press, 1998.

Gay, Kathlyn. *Church and State.* Brookfield, CT: Millbrook Press, 1992.

Hass, Carol. *Engel v. Vitale: Separation of Church and State* (Landmark Supreme Court Cases). Berkeley Heights, NJ: Enslow Publishers, 1994.

Jacoby, Susan. *Freethinkers: A History of American Secularism.* New York: Metropolitan Books, 2004.

Levert, Suzanne. *The Supreme Court.* New York: Benchmark Books, 2002.

Loren, Julia C. *Engel v. Vitale: Prayer in the Public Schools* (Famous Trials). San Diego: Lucent Books, 2000.

Patrick, John J. *The Bill of Rights: A History in Documents* (Pages from History). New York: Oxford University Press, 2003.

_____. *The Supreme Court of the United States: A Student Companion* (Oxford Student Companions to American Government), second ed. New York: Oxford University Press, 2002.

Peters, Shawn Francis. *Judging Jehovah's Witnesses: Religious Persecution And the Dawn of the Rights Revolution*. Lawrence: University Press of Kansas, 2002.

Sherrow, Victoria. *Separation of Church and State*. New York: Franklin Watts, 1992.

Wacker, Grant. *Religion in 19th Century America* (Religion in American Life). New York: Oxford University Press, 2000.

Wagman, Robert J., *The First Amendment Book*. New York: World Almanac, 1991.

Weiss, Ann E. *God and Government: The Separation of Church and State*. Boston: Houghton Mifflin Company, 1990.

WEB SITES

Administrative Office of the U.S. Courts.
http://www.uscourts.gov/

Avalon Project at Yale Law School, Documents in Law, History and Diplomacy.
http://www.yale.edu/lawweb/avalon/avalon.htm

FindLaw, U.S. Supreme Court decisions.
http://www.findlaw.com/casecode/supreme.html

Iowa Court Information System.
http://www.judicial.state.ia.us/students/6/

Junto Society, "Presidential inaugural speeches."
http://www.juntosociety.com/inaugural/jadams.html

Legal Information Institute, Cornell Law School.
www.law.cornell.edu/constitution/constitution.billofrights.html

The Library of Congress, American Memory site.
http://memory.loc.gov/ammem/

Library of Congress's Thomas: Legislative Information on the Internet.
http://thomas.loc.gov

National Museum of American Jewish History.
http://nmajh.org/

Oyez, U.S. Supreme Court Multimedia site.
http://www.oyez.org/oyez/frontpage

School of Law, Emory, Macmillan Law Library. Amendments to the Constitution.
http://www.law.emory.edu/FEDERAL/usconst/amend.html

Supreme Court Historical Society.
http://www.supremecourthistory.org

Supreme Court of the United States site.
http://www.supremecourtus.gov

U.S. Constitution Online,
http://www.usconstitution.net.

U.S. Government Printing Office.
http://www.gpoaccess.gov/constitution/browse.html. Last updated: September 15, 2004.

U.S. National Archives & Records Administration, Federal Register. "The Constitutional Amendment Process."
http://www.archives.gov/federal_register/constitution/amendment_process.html.

All Web sites accessible as of October 18, 2004.

TEACHERS' GUIDES

National Association of Criminal Defense Lawyers
Includes a lesson plan on Gideon At 40.
www.nacdl.org

Street Law
Provides lesson plans on twenty landmark Supreme Court Cases.
www.streetlaw.com

BIBLIOGRAPHY

ARTICLES

Americans United For Separation of Church and State. "Is America A 'Christian Nation', Religion, Government And Individual Freedom." http://www.au.org/site/DocServer/Is_the_United_States_a_ Christian_nation.pdf?docID=103.

"The Bible in the Schools," *The New York Times*, Nov. 29, 1871.

"Bill of Rights in Action," Constitutional Rights Foundation, Spring 1991, vol. 7, issue 4.

Brumberg, Stephan F. "The Cincinnati Bible War," *HUC Journal*, vol. LIV.2 April 29, 2004.

Byrne, Julie. "Roman Catholics and Immigration in Nineteenth-Century America," National Humanities Center.
http://www.nhc.rtp.nc.us:8080/tserve/nineteen/nkeyinfo/nromcath .htm.

"CBS Reports: Storm Over the Supreme Court," March 13, 1963, transcript, cited in *The Constitution: That Delicate Balance*. by Fred W. Friendly and Martha J. H. Elliot. New York: Random House, 1984.

"Court dismisses Pledge case," CNN, June 15, 2004.

"Debate 6—Prayer in Public Schools." Pearson/Prentice Hall. http://www.graves.k12.ky.us/schools/GCHS/bleonard/HTML/d/ debate6.htm.

DeWan, George. "School Prayer Divides LI," *Newsday*, 2004.

Dunn, Susan. "The Inquisition in Alabama." *Christian Science Monitor*, August 28, 2003.

Green, Steven Keith. "The National Reform Association and the Religious Amendments to the Constitution, 1864–1876." An unpublished Masters thesis, University of North Carolina at Chapel Hill, 1987.

"High court: Atheist can't challenge 'God' in Pledge," Associated Press, June 14, 2004.

Israelite, January 8, 1869, p. 4, cited in "The Cincinnati Bible War," Stephan F. Brumberg, *HUC Journal*, vol. LIV.2, April 29, 2004.

Jones, Jeffrey Owen. "The Pledge's Creator." *The Smithsonian Magazine*, November 2003.

Kirkpatrick, David. "THE 2004 CAMPAIGN: THE TACTICS; Republicans Admit Mailing Campaign Literature Saying Liberals Will Ban the Bible," *The New York Times*, September 24, 2004.

Kurtzman, Daniel. "News Analysis: School–Religion Amendment Fails, But the Fight Is Long from Finished," *Jewish Telegraphic Agency*, June 12, 1998.

Lewis, Anthony. "Court Again Under Fire," *The New York Times*, July 1, 1962.

———. "Supreme Court Outlaws Official School Prayers in Regents Case Decision," *The New York Times*, June 25, 1962.

McAndrews, Lawrence J. "'Moral' Victories: Ronald Reagan and the Debate over School Prayer," *Religion & Education*, vol. 30, no. 1. Spring 2003.

"Maryland Backs Prayer in School; Baltimore Practice Upheld by State High Court, 4 to 3 Two Amendments Cited Chief Judge Dissents New York Prayer Upheld," *The New York Times*, April 7, 1962.

"National Organizations Oppose Istook Amendment," Religious Action Center of Reform Judaism, March 3, 1998.

Nieves, Evelyn, "Judges Ban Pledge of Allegiance From Schools, Citing 'Under God,'" *The New York Times*, June 27, 2002.

"A Radical Assault on the Constitution," *The New York Times*, July 24, 2004.

"Religion and the Founding of the American Republic," Library of Congress. http://www.loc.gov/exhibits/religion.

Silver, Roy R. "5 L.I. Parents Who Started Suit Hail Decision," *The New York Times*, June 26, 1962.

Stout, David. "Court Ruling Keeps Pledge Intact but Leaves 'God' Issue Unsettled." *The New York Times*, June 14, 2004.

Totenberg, Nina. "Profile: Papers of Former Supreme Court Justice Harry Blackmun," National Public Radio, March 7, 2004.

Weart, William G. "Bible in Schools Curbed by Court." *The New York Times*, Feb. 2, 1962.

"William J. Butler." Urban Morgan Institute for Human Rights, Cincinnati, Ohio. http://www.law.uc.edu/morgan/butler01/butlerbio.html.

Zimmerman, Jonathan. "The Other Massive Resistance: School Prayer and the Conservative Revolution, 1962–1984." New York University, January 25, 2001.

AUTHOR'S INTERVIEW
Author's interview with Bertram B. Daiker, September 1, 2004.

BOOKS
Ahlstrom, Sydney E. A. *Religious History of the American People*. New Haven: Yale University Press, 1972.

Alley, Robert S. *School Prayer: The Court, the Congress, and the First Amendment*. New York: Prometheus Books, 1994.

The Bible in the Public Schools. Arguments Before the Superior Court of Cincinnati in the Case of Minor v. Board of Education of Cincinnati *(1870) with the Opinions of the Court and the Opinion on Appeal of the Supreme Court of Ohio*. New York: Da Capo Press, 1967.

Boston, Rob. *Why the Religious Right is Wrong About Separation of Church and State*. Amherst, NY: Prometheus Books, 1994.

Burnham, Alexander. "Edict Is Called a Setback by Christian Clerics Rabbis Praise It; Churchmen Voice Shock at Ruling," *The New York Times*, June 26, 1962, p.7.

Colcord, Willard, ed. *American State Papers Bearing on Sunday Legislation*. Washington, D.C.: The Religious Liberty Association, 1911.

DelFattore, Joan. *The Fourth R: Conflicts Over Religion in America's Public Schools*. New Haven, Connecticut: Yale University Press, 2004.

Friendly, Fred W., and Martha J. H. Elliott. *The Constitution: That Delicate Balance*. New York: Random House, 1984.

Haught, James. *2000 Years of Disbelief: Famous People With the Courage to Doubt*. Amherst, NY: Prometheus Books, 1996.

Howe, Mark DeWolfe. *The Garden and the Wilderness: Religion and Government in American Constitutional History*. Chicago: University of Chicago Press, 1965.

Ivers, Gregg. *To Build a Wall: American Jews and the Separation of Church and State*. Charlottesville,University Press of Virginia, 1995.

Kurland, Philip B., and Gerhard Casper. *Landmark Briefs and Arguments of the Supreme Court of the United States: Constitutional Law,* "Engel v. Vitale," vol. 56. Arlington, VA: University Publications of America Inc., 1975.

Lieberman, Jethro K. *Milestones! Two Hundred Years of American Law*. New York: Oxford University Press, 1976.

Link, Arthur S., Robert V. Remini, Douglas Greenberg, and Robert C. McMath Jr. *A Concise History of the American People*. Arlington Heights, IL: Harlan Davidson, 1984.

McCollum, Vashti Cromwell. *One Woman's Fight*. Madison, WI: Freedom From Religion Foundation Inc., 1993.

Morse, Samuel F. B. *Imminent Dangers to the Free Institutions of the United States Through Foreign Immigration (1835)*. New York: Arno Press, Inc., 1969.

Nelson, William E. *Marbury v. Madison: The Origins and Legacy of Judicial Review*. Lawrence: University Press of Kansas, 2000.

O'Brien, David M. *Animal Sacrifice and Religious Freedom:* Church of the Lukumi Babalu Aye *v.* City of Hialeah. Lawrence: University Press of Kansas, 2004.

Pfeffer, Leo. *Church, State, and Freedom*. Boston: Beacon Press, 1967.

Platner, John Winthrop, William W. Fenn, et al. *The Religious History of New England*. Cambridge, Massachusetts: Harvard University Press, 1917.

Shawn, Francis. *Judging the Jehovah's Wittnesses: Religious Persecution and the Dawn of the Rights Revolution*. Lawrence: University Press of Kansas, 2000.

Sherrow, Victoria. *Separation of Church and State*. New York: Franklin Watts, 1992.

"Supreme Court of the United States," booklet. Washington, D.C.: Supreme Court Historical Society.

Weiss, Ann E. *God and Government: The Separation of Church and State*. Boston: Houghton Mifflin, 1982.

Wicker, Tom. *Dwight D. Eisenhower*. New York: Times Books/Henry Holt & Company, 2002.

STATUTES/COURT CASES/DOCUMENTS

Abington School District v. *Schempp*, 374 U.S. 203 (1963).

Address of the Danbury Baptist Association in the State of Connecticut assembled October 7, 1801, to Thomas Jefferson, Esq., President of the United States of America.

Allegheny v. *ACLU* 492 U.S., 573 (1989). Articles of Confederation.

Barbary Treaties: Treaty of Peace and Friendship, Signed at Tripoli November 4, 1796.

A Bill Establishing a Provision for Teachers of the Christian Religion. Proposed by Patrick Henry in the Virginia legislature, 1784.

Davis v. *Beason*, 133 US 333 (1890).

Elk Grove Unified School District and David W. Gordon v. *Michael A. Newdow et al*, No. 02--1624.

Engel v. *Vitale*, 370 U.S. 421 (1962),

Everson v. *Board of Education of Ewing TP*., 330 U.S. 1 (1947).

"Expressing the sense of Congress that schools in the United States should set aside a sufficient period of time to allow children to pray for, or quietly reflect on behalf of, the Nation during this time of struggle against the forces of international terrorism." H. CON. RES. 239.

First Amendment.

Fourteenth Amendment.

Gitlow v. *New York*, 268 US 652 (1925).

H.CON.RES.239. http://thomas.loc.gov/cgi-bin/bdquery/z?d107:h. con.res.00239:

House Rpt.105—543—"Proposing an Amendment to the Constitution of the United States Restoring Religious Freedom." http://thomas .loc.gov/cgi-bin/cpquery/?&db_id=cp105&r_n=hr543.105&sel =TOC_65852&

Jefferson, Thomas. "Bill for Establishing Religious Freedom," 1786.

———. Letter to the Danbury Baptist Association, January 1, 1802.

Lee v. *Weisman*, 505 U.S. 577 (1992).

Letter of John Adams to Benjamin Rush, June 12, 1812, quoted in *The Spur of Fame*, J. A. Schutz and D. Adair, eds. San Marino, CA: The Huntington Library, 1966.

McCollum v. *Board of Education*, 333 U.S. 203 (1948).

Madison, James. "Memorial and Remonstrance, 1785."

Michael A. Newdow v. *Elk Grove Unified School District et al*, United States Court of Appeals for the Ninth Circuit, No. 00-16423.

Minersville School District v. *Gobitis*, 310 U.S. 586 (1940).

Paine, Thomas. *Age of Reason* (1795).

———. "Declaration of the Rights of Man" (1789).

People ex rel. Ring v. *Board of Education*, 245 Ill. 334, 351 (1910).

Permoli v. *Municipality No. 1 of the City of New Orleans*, 44 U.S. 589 (1845).

"Proposing an amendment to the Constitution of the United States restoring religious freedom. H. J. RES. 46." Library of Congress.

"Providing for Consideration of H.R. 3313, Marriage Protection Act of 2004," House of Representatives, July 22, 2004, Congressional Record, p. H6569

"Regents' Prayer," *Engel* v. *Vitale*, 370 U.S. 421 (1962).

Reynolds v. *United States*, 98 U.S. 145 (1878).

Santa Fe Independent School District v. *Doe* (99—62) 530 U.S. 290 (2000).

Seixas, Moses. "Letter to President George Washington," 1789.

Slaughter—House Cases, 83 U.S. 36 (1872).

Stone v. *Graham*, 449 U.S. 39 (1980).

U.S. Constitution.

U.S. Representative Ernest J. Istook Jr. "Detailed and Legal Analysis Of the Religious Freedom Amendment House Joint Resolution 78."

Wallace v. *Jaffree*, 472 U.S. 38 (1985).

Washington, George. "Letter to Touro Synagogue," 1789.

———. Thanksgiving Proclamation, 1789.

West Virginia State Board of Education v. *Barnette*, 319 US 624 (1943).

Wisconsin v. *Yoder*, 406 U.S. 205 (1972).

"Words and Deeds in American History," Letter, Billy Gobitas to Minersville, Pennsylvania, school directors, explaining why the young Jehovah's Witness refused to salute the American flag, 5 November 1935. (William Gobitas Papers), Library of Congress, http://memory.loc.gov/ammem.

Zorach v. *Clauson*, 343 U.S. 306 (1952).

index

about the author

SUSAN DUDLEY GOLD has written more than three dozen books for middle-school and high-school students on a variety of topics, including American history, health issues, law, and space. Her most recent works for Marshall Cavendish Benchmark are *Gun Control* in the Open for Debate series, and *Roe v. Wade: A Woman's Choice?*, *Brown v. Board of Education: Special but Equal?*, and *The Pentagon Papers: National Security or the Right to Know*—all in the Supreme Court Milestones series. She is currently working on two more books about Supreme Court cases.

Gold has also written several books on Maine history. Among her many careers in journalism are stints as a reporter for a daily newspaper, managing editor of two statewide business magazines, and freelance writer for several regional publications. She and her husband, John Gold, own and operate a Web design and publishing business. Susan has received numerous awards for her writing and design work. Susan and her husband, also a children's book author, live in Maine. They have one son, Samuel.